I Am the Gift —

Everyday Inspirations that Empower

*A positive focus on the gifts we are
provided as women; learning to understand
and accept the strength we possess to
enlighten others through ourselves as
The Gift*

**Carol Lynn Pasewark, MEd, LPC
and friends**

*The final forming of a person's character
lies in their own hands.—Anne Frank*

Publisher: Carol Lynn Pasewark
clpasewark@live.com

ISBN 978-0-578-03100-2

Printed in the United States of America

First Printing July 2009

FOREWORD

This book is dedicated first to my daughters in the hope they will find and embrace a sense of self that provides them with an assurance only found in personal power as a woman. My sincere and loving hope is they avoid some of the painful mistakes I have experienced in relationships and life in general.

Helen Keller wrote that true happiness is not attained through self-gratification but through fidelity to a worthy purpose. Do you have purpose in your life? My purpose here is to enlighten others in the way I have been enlightened, and yes it is very fulfilling. Many of the writings reflect a developing understanding of my personal power as a woman. They represent the changes I have made in my life, over time and through struggles.

It is my hope that the daily support offered through the inspirations and your reflections will guide you to not only find but embrace your personal power. In using this book, you may discover your power as that of becoming a stronger person, more assertive and assured in your place as a woman. Some may have the desire to become dominant in your relationships. The reflection page of the book is meant to help discover the way in which you choose to express your new understanding of this power. How you use it is up to you. The book is not meant to diminish anyone's role in life, only to enhance it.

However you find yourself in these readings, it is my ardent hope that you share what you learn of yourself with other women. We have strength that needs nurturing; a unique wisdom to share, a spirit that can embolden and enrich so many lives, and the heart of lioness protecting her cubs. Let us reach out to each other and combine our resources to provide our society with the gifts they are so desperately needed. For it is true, *I AM THE GIFT.*

Thought for the day

I am the gift. What a concept! Throughout history men have desired and women have been desired by them. When I understand and accept that I am the gift, I am able to act accordingly. I can remember a time when my thinking centered on what I needed to do, who I needed to be in order to attract that certain man. I now see the fallacy in this thinking. It is more important that I learn to be myself, and in appreciating that uniqueness I look for who may be worthy of what I have to offer, not the other way around. These are new ideas to me and I am sometimes uncomfortable with them. However, I do believe them and know them to be true. Past ideas have held me hostage and caused me to allow treatment that is so less than I deserve. The time for change has come. Act accordingly.

Meditation for the day

My focus for the day is the gifts I have to offer making me the best gift of all. I reflect on past events only long enough to recognize how they have distorted my thinking and self-image today. I then bring to my awareness the convergence of spirit, mind, and temperament and relinquish the fears of the past.

Prayer for the day

Thou who art eternal, guide and strengthen us this day. Temper our newfound strength with a humility that allows us to see ourselves for the gift we are. Provide us with a new comfort in our ideas of self-consideration and please give us confidence to accept the gift you have given, the gift of self.

Mantra for the day

I have confidence and comfort in my place as the gift. I have confidence and comfort in my place as the gift.

Reflection for the day

_____

_____

_____

_____

_____

_____

_____

_____

_____

_____

_____

_____

_____

_____

_____

_____

_____

_____

Thought for the day

The strength and courage that most women possess can be an overwhelming force to many people. Our history of servitude and matronly roles has conspired against us to suppress our true power. This strength can be intimidating, even to other women. Therefore, it is important to understand that real change comes slowly and genuinely. This change is accomplished not by burning bras and fighting the established way of society, but by patience, courage and compassion. This does not mean we turn our backs on the natural gifts of hospitality and motherly intuition that come so easily to most of us. It just means that these roles do not define or limit us. We expand our thinking and our emotions to define ourselves in the way we choose without feelings of expectation or duty.

Meditation for the day

I nourish all areas of my life to include, but not be limited by, traditional roles as I see them play out in my life. I add to my repertoire by seeking new avenues of expression and using these to my benefit and the well-being of others.

Prayer for the day

I pray to have the grace and strength to accept my natural abilities as they are. I will not allow society's ideas to limit my thinking and aspirations. I seek to contribute to mine, and other women's abilities to expand our sphere of positive contribution.

Mantra for the day

Like the diamond, I have many facets. I cultivate all aspects for a stronger perspective on myself and life. Like the diamond, I have many facets. I cultivate all aspects for a stronger perspective on myself and life.

Reflection for the day

_____

_____

_____

_____

_____

_____

_____

_____

_____

_____

_____

_____

_____

_____

_____

_____

Thought for the day

It seems that whenever I go through a romantic break up I doubt myself, my self-esteem drops and I question my worth. When it ends and I'm broken-hearted, I need to remember this simple truth. The lover has not rejected me personally; they have rejected their willingness to love. They have denounced their most fundamental and joyous of human rights; the right to love. The desire not to bond with me is a reflection of their fears and inabilities, not mine. I have taken the chance on romance once again. I have been willing to exercise my rights. I have relied on faith to bring us together not the fear that drives us apart. I have lived my faith.

Meditation for the day

I need to focus on who I am and the attributes that I possess. The fact that I am willing and able to love speaks of my spiritual growth. I look to the faith I've exercised and the love that I am willing to share. I realize that I am doing what my God would have me do; love. My love will be shared and enjoyed by someone more spiritually evolved.

Prayer for the day

I pray that I stay near my God, the One who always graciously receives my love.

Mantra for the day

I claim my right to love. I claim my right to love. I claim my right to love.

Reflection for the day

_____

_____

_____

_____

_____

_____

_____

_____

_____

_____

_____

_____

_____

_____

_____

_____

_____

_____

Thought for the day

There is no energy crisis! Even though my body sometimes feels fatigue, my mind has the unlimited capacity to accept and discharge energy. First and foremost, I must come to believe that this energy exists. Secondly, I need to realize that I have access to all the energy of the universe, as does everyone else. Third, I will disseminate the positive from the negative energy available. Finally, I will rebuff all negative energy and be left with only positive pure energy to use for the betterment of all. Whatever I apply my energy to will grow. This is where I must be careful. My present and future depend on my choices of where the energy will be applied. Spiritual energy, like money or emotion must be used wisely, effectively, and unselfishly. I am grateful to know that I am kindness and wisdom.

Meditation for the day

I ponder the sagacious use of my resources. I am in command of my energy. I will not let another rob me of my universal due. Through prayer and interaction with my community I gather the insight I need to make wise choices for the allocation of my spiritual assets.

Prayer for the day

I pray to be a righteous steward of the potentiality and spirit available to me. I ask for wisdom and kindness to be my guide in the distribution of positive forces.

Mantra for the day

I am power, wisdom and energy. I am power, wisdom and energy. I am power wisdom and energy.

Reflection for the day

_____

_____

_____

_____

_____

_____

_____

_____

_____

_____

_____

_____

_____

_____

_____

_____

Thought for the day

It's been said that life is not a dress rehearsal. I've spent a good deal of my life waiting for things to happen. I've been waiting for employment opportunities, waiting for the right partner and waiting for the right relationship. Well, the wait is over. I am now officially into action! I've thought about life long enough, I've made enough plans, I've tolerated enough inactivity, both from myself and others. Today is the day that I apply my considerable talents and education to create the life I've been longing for. When I marshal all of my resources and fortify my efforts with prayer I will be able to promote the changes I've only dreamed of.

Meditation for the day

Today I do not contemplate the past, other people's doubts or my fears. I meditate on my goals and make sure no one, including myself, stands in the way of the changes that I am implementing. I apply the positive power of meditation to my dreams and allow my new found power to flow through me. With the love of God and the people in my life, we can do anything. Change is mine!

Prayer for the day

I acknowledge through prayer that the rehearsal of this life has prepared me for a place center stage and in the spotlight. I deserve good things. People have always said I deserve better, I've always wanted better and I'm positive that my God can and will provide better. Together we are strong!

Mantra for the day

Rehearsal is over; my life has begun. Rehearsal is over; my life has begun. Rehearsal is over; life has begun.

Reflection for the day

_____

_____

_____

_____

_____

_____

_____

_____

_____

_____

_____

_____

_____

_____

_____

_____

_____

_____

Thought for the day

For many of us, learning to change the way we think is like learning a new language. At first it makes no sense, we don't see the connection between what we know and what we are learning. We say the new word, spell the new word, even write it, but we still hear what we know in our heads. It is said that when you can think in another language is when you really know it. It's like that with changing old ideas as well. It takes time and much practice. If my perseverance wanes, the old thinking dominates. Decide the change you want to occur in your thinking and begin the practice of learning the new language of your mind.

Meditation for the day

My focus today is practice, practice, practice. I am changing things about myself to reflect a more positive woman. It begins in my mind. The new language I am learning will take time but the more I use it, the more it will become part of who I am.

Prayer for the day

I pray for perseverance in efforts to change my thinking. I ask for wisdom and patience in my endeavor of growth. I am lacking nothing, through God's Grace, and will reflect that in my thinking daily.

Mantra for the day

I am growing with the practice of the new language in my thinking. I am growing with the practice of the new language in my thinking.

Reflection for the day

_____

_____

_____

_____

_____

_____

_____

_____

_____

_____

_____

_____

_____

_____

_____

_____

_____

Thought for the day

Whenever we are faced with a fear we can surrender to it, flee from it or try to control it. Men fear women for they recognize a woman's strength, spiritual connection and sensual power. Men are often envious of a woman's ability to feel and share her emotions. Many cultures and religions sanction the covering of the female body for if she is covered, her sensuality will be restrained. This is not an attempt to save the woman's dignity but rather, to limit her impact on the men and the emotions that they have difficulty expressing. Non-committal men run not from the woman but from themselves. They will have their fun until things get serious (emotional) then they need to flee. They emotionally back away for their fear will not allow them to move forward. This only leaves surrender to the woman as the only viable option for a man to learn to live a life that is truly emotionally fulfilling. He will not learn fulfillment from his buddies in the locker room for they have the same flee or control mentality.

Meditation for the day

I view myself in a new light regarding relationships. I will realize my true worth as the foundation for emotional guidance and peace. When I can make surrender an appealing option I can provide the safety that he needs to begin his spiritual and emotional transformation. My love, direction and patience are my gift to man.

Prayer for the day

I ask the Creator for the strength and wisdom to make my life appealing. I ask that others be attracted by my intellect and peace and seek me out for Greater guidance.

Mantra for the day
     I am emotionally attractive. I am emotionally attractive. I am emotionally attractive.

Reflection for the day

_____

_____

_____

_____

_____

_____

_____

_____

_____

_____

_____

_____

_____

_____

_____

_____

_____

Thought for the day

The loneliness and sadness that we feel when separated from loved ones is merely a reflection of our separation from our Creator. The separation from our loved ones can be either time, distance or emotional. However, the feelings and actions are the same. We consciously try to control the power of love. Sometimes we restrict our feelings when we are angry at a loved one. Perhaps we won't speak with them or find some other punitive measure to levy against them in an attempt to make us feel better. Sometimes we resist the power of love as a way to ease our pain. Or worse still, we devalue the other person so we can feel better about ourselves. Whenever we resist or restrict the flow of love we are shutting ourselves off from the love of our Creator. It is doubtful that you can remove yourself from the love of man without removing yourself from the love of God.

Meditation for the day

Whom do I hurt? Whom do I harm when I choose to distance myself emotionally from others? This is the type of self-righteous masochism that I am trying to avoid. No one is excluded from the loving touch of our Creator, so I too will adopt a no exclusion rule to aid myself in my personal and spiritual growth.

Prayer for the day

Today I ask that I be divorced from the malicious thoughts that separate me from God's children. I pray to see that as humans we are all of one family, and I need to find a loving place in that family. I ask that even though I may be temporarily distraught, I make no conscious effort to restrict the Divine flow of love.

Mantra for the day
      I will not restrict the flow of love. I will not restrict the flow of love. I will not restrict the flow of love.

Reflection for the day

_____

_____

_____

_____

_____

_____

_____

_____

_____

_____

_____

_____

_____

_____

Thought for the day

We are all someone's daughter. We may have a different structure in our family; legally adopted, heartfully adopted, or natural. It is important to pass on the knowledge of the older and wiser to the younger and innocent, less-experienced ones. The problem is we don't listen. We think we know better, we think the older and wiser mother is far removed from the problems of the day. Everything is cyclical. Experiences are not lost to the generations, they are repeated. It may have a slightly different face or name, but the struggle is the same. Am I lovable, will I succeed in life, can I make a meaningful contribution? The way we see things changes over time and experience. Learn to listen and apply what you hear. Believe your mother loves you more than anything and wants only the best for you always. Trust that.

Meditation for the day

I ponder the messages given me by my life-giver. My focus will be on what my mother wants for me, the best always. I will remember the love that is so genuinely and freely given and learn how to show myself the same consideration and love.

Prayer for the day

I pray to listen well. I pray to ponder these experiences of my heart for my benefit and for the good of those around me. I ask to pass on to my daughter the knowledge that is so lovingly given to me.

Mantra for the day

I am special. I am the daughter of a strong woman that loves me and wants my best. I am special.

Reflection for the day

_____

_____

_____

_____

_____

_____

_____

_____

_____

_____

_____

_____

_____

_____

_____

_____

_____

_____

Thought for the day

Soothe yourself. Pay attention to your needs. Pamper yourself for a change. You are worthy of love and nurturing. We spend an inordinate amount of time tending to the demands and expectations of others while discounting our own. When things get out of balance, we begin to slight ourselves and our yearnings. Soak in the warmth of the fire, breathe in the sweet aroma of the flowers, listen to the songbirds with a new appreciation, and allow the touch of the chenille blanket to caress your skin. What do you really want to do for yourself right now? Give yourself permission and go for it. You are worthy.

Meditation for the day

Today I focus on my senses and all the joy they bring to me. I ask myself what I desire and give myself permission to indulge. I focus on the love I have for myself knowing that by enriching my own life, I therefore enrich those around me as well. I find acceptance that I am worthy of the devotion and care I often extend only to others.

Prayer for the day

I ask for a sense of self-care that often eludes me. In this, I pray for relief from inauthentic guilt that can accompany a desire to meet my needs first. Help me to remember that as I care for myself, I set an example and extend my benefit to others.

Mantra for the day

I am worthy of devotion and care. I am
worthy of devotion and care. I am worthy of
devotion and care.

Reflection for the day

_____

_____

_____

_____

_____

_____

_____

_____

_____

_____

_____

_____

_____

_____

_____

_____

_____

Thought for the day

The ego is a powerful enemy in one's search for personal enlightenment. I have heard the old acronym for ego as being **E**dging **G**od **O**ut. We can see that if we are acting on self-will and self-determination we will certainly be edging God out. My challenge is to keep my ego in check. It does not matter if my ego seeks to tell me that I am wonderful or horrible; it is still a negative exercise in self. Anything I do to distance myself from man will distance me from my Creator. I shall seek to be fair with my own assessment, equal with others and humble before my Creator. It is only by taking an accurate appraisal of myself that I can accomplish my goals of humility and usefulness. Today I work to continue my journey toward humility and enlightenment.

Meditation for the day

This day's reflection calls me to find my proper size in the universe. True leaders guide with assurance for they have the humility to walk under the Grace. Humility, emotional stability and a loving heart will give me the qualities that I seek to be most useful.

Prayer for the day

A humble person maintains a spiritual connection. I take time throughout this day to check in with the Great Spirit for continued guidance and purpose. The strength of my spirituality contributes to my humility and usefulness.

Mantra for the day

I seek a humble heart. I seek a humble heart. I seek a humble heart.

Reflection for the day

_____

_____

_____

_____

_____

_____

_____

_____

_____

_____

_____

_____

_____

_____

_____

_____

_____

Thought for the day

I need to resist the socialization efforts to get me to see this life as a competition. Television, radio and newspapers all celebrate the winners and cast off the losers only to find a new and brighter winner next week. BULLSHIT! I will not give up on the idea that we are all winners and that no one needs to be excluded. Life is not a competition, it is an opportunity. When the world tricks us into competing with each other it is for their benefit not ours. I've never read any spiritual principles based on competition. It seems that the Great Spirit created needs in each of us that others can help us fulfill; we need each other. When we work from an exclusionary perspective our world gets smaller, less productive, and lonelier. When I unselfishly work to satisfy a heart there is no competition only love. Love is the greatest opportunity we will ever have. Our primary purpose is to learn to love and take the opportunities afforded to share it.

Meditation for the day

I seek to be useful in the distribution of kindness and love. I seize my opportunities to freely share and leave the competitions of man to those less enlightened. Competition brings no genuine victory. We were born with all that we need. A full heart and the blessings of a kind and loving Creator will sustain me.

Prayer for the day

I pray to be free from the pettiness of man. I ask to be given the level of compassion that I will need to be of service to my Maker. I seek wisdom to fulfill my destiny as a child of God and a loving woman to all. I pray to stay focused on my spiritual life and remain useful.

Mantra for the day
      It is an opportunity not a competition. It is an opportunity not a competition. It is an opportunity not a competition.

Reflection for the day

_____

_____

_____

_____

_____

_____

_____

_____

_____

_____

_____

_____

_____

_____

_____

Thought for the Day

Being a pioneer in the evolution of women, I must realize that I have no comparison. I often stand alone in my beliefs and actions. There is no one in history to show me the way to the new land. This is why it is so important to find other like-minded women; women, who like myself, believe that the old ways will continue to destroy the planet and everyone on it. The women I seek know and realize in the depths of their being that love is the answer. Women who are patient enough to listen, bold enough to speak up and diligent enough to work for change. These women are my heroes, they are also my peers for we are working together to build a better, more loving world. As leaders, we walk with our heads held high and our vision focused only on the future.

Meditation for the Day

Even though I get disappointed, my heart will not be dominated by hardness and cynicism. I am a woman of love and I will bring that love into all I do. I will stay flexible and meet the challenges of life with a kind heart and a visionary spirit.

Prayer for the Day

I ask for continued strength to meet the goals that I set for myself. I ask that Divine inspiration be acquired and shared by others so that we can better the world and ourselves. My prayer is for peace, love and the inspiration to promote change.

Mantra for the Day

       I am a pioneer. I am a pioneer. I am a pioneer.

Reflection for the day

_____

_____

_____

_____

_____

_____

_____

_____

_____

_____

_____

_____

_____

_____

_____

_____

_____

_____

Thought for the day

   We have talked much about helping others. We have also explored the concept of self-promotion. This would appear to be a dichotomous belief system. Life, by its nature, is disjointed. Let's hope that we never head in a straight and unwavering direction! What differentiates these two concepts is intent. I can promote myself through selfishness or like an enlightened woman through self-awareness. The first seeks self for self's sake and personal gain. The second seeks a promotion of self to become aware of the needs of others. When I promote myself today, it is to become more aware of my goodness, graciousness and power. My so-called self-promotion is for the benefit of all; for when I have power I have power to share. As I grow, my capacity to empower others and lift them from their present circumstances grows as well. There is a never-ending source of Power to which I have access and it is my privilege to unselfishly share it.

Meditation for the day

   I consider my intent and motives. Is my desire for self awareness and personal power really for the benefit of all or is it a selfish pursuit? People are drawn to me therefore I need my motives to be pure for I seek to promote Glory, not the sickness of self.

Prayer for the day

   I sincerely ask for purity of thought, word, and deed. Today I will promote myself though my efforts and with the kindness of others. I ask that I use my newfound self-awareness and power for the good of all.

Mantra for the day

I am self-aware not self-important. I am self-aware not self-important. I am self-aware not self-important.

Reflection for the day

_____

_____

_____

_____

_____

_____

_____

_____

_____

_____

_____

_____

_____

_____

_____

_____

_____

_____

Thought for the Day

We were taught to always put the other person in our relationship first. We were told to work for their happiness at the expense of ours. This self-sacrificing behavior accounts for the current status of women throughout the world. Women are not second-class citizens! In truth there are no second-class citizens. We are all free to grow as we will and to share with others as circumstances warrant. There are leaders and followers. If I find peace in following then I should gleefully submit. However, if I am a woman with latent leadership skills I need to bring them to the forefront to find my wholeness. The only peace that I'll find is the peace that I create. There are plenty of men who long to follow the dictates of a strong, independent woman. When I claim my right to lead, they can claim their peace and glory in submission to me. In this way everyone can be happy and at peace. I'm not here to rail against people or to get lost in power struggles. I am here to, first and foremost, meet my needs and allow others into my life as it benefits me. I, and I alone, am responsible for my happiness and well-being.

Meditation for the Day

How often have I traded my power and dignity in an effort to find my power and dignity? Once I realize that this woman was born to live to her full advantage, the fairy tales of my youth fall by the wayside. I will reflect on the fallacy of trying to find happiness through submission. It just doesn't become me!

Prayer for the Day

I pray to fully realize that I can do this. I can run my life to my advantage and feel good about it. I pray to be free from guilt of my past as I change my interactions with the world

Mantra for the day

I am first at last! I am first at last! I am first at last!

Reflection for the day

_____

_____

_____

_____

_____

_____

_____

_____

_____

_____

_____

_____

_____

_____

Thought for the day

We strive to be equal in our personal relationships; however, this is not a viable concept. Name one other relationship that you have that is equal. The boss has power over you. You have power over children and certain family members. Friends have a hierarchy based on social status. Equality does not exist. Yet, we've been told to strive for parity in our romantic relationships. Perhaps this is just a patriarchal ploy to forestall the inevitable rise of matriarchy. When we refuse to relegate our power to men, we reinforce our place of authority. As women of change we must banish the fetters of the past, rebuff the resistance of the day and live in our potentiality. We must claim our rightful place as head of the household. The unenlightened male will in time gladly accept a subordinate position to the woman of the home. It is in this position of service that his true potential as a male can be achieved.

Meditation for the day

Today I visualize my potential as a queen. I see my new household and I rule it with satisfaction and harmony. The gifts are mine to receive, the universe has placed woman in the leadership role, and I need to claim my privilege.

Prayer for the day

I pray to recognize my power today. I ask to be made aware of how and with whom I choose to share my strength. I pray for a humble heart that can claim what is rightfully mine. I ask God for guidance to make this transition of power a positive experience for all concerned.

Mantra for the day

The queen claims that which is hers. She guides with love. The queen claims that which is hers. She guides with love. The queen claims that which is hers.

Reflection for the day

_____

_____

_____

_____

_____

_____

_____

_____

_____

_____

_____

_____

_____

_____

_____

_____

_____

Thought for the day

Self-esteem is always a popular topic with many different views and perspectives. Some people say that self-esteem is what I think of myself, others say it is what I <u>think</u> they think of me. I find both of these concepts to be erroneous; otherwise I would think far better of myself than I do. It is easy to see how I could have an occluded picture of myself given the contradictory concepts that abound. I've always thought reasonably well of myself. However, what I think they think of me is incongruent with the truth. Once more I find that my own dishonest and negative thinking has disrupted my forward progress by accepting false perceptions as truth. When I clear my mind of negativity I am truly able to view myself as God views me. I KNOW what God thinks of me. In my Higher Power I find an endless supply of comfort, joy, love and understanding that truly defines my worth to myself and others.

Meditation for the day

Today and forevermore I seek to be free from misperceptions of self. I glory in my personal accomplishments and the joy and comfort that I bring into the lives of those that I love. <u>It is what I do that defines my worth, not what I think!</u>

Prayer for the day

I pray to be a woman of action. I pray to quiet the negative self-talk that insists that I believe less of myself. I pray to let the love of my God and my positive actions define my worth.

Mantra for the day

I do not need earthly validation. I do not need earthly validation. I do not need earthly validation.

Reflection for the day

_____

_____

_____

_____

_____

_____

_____

_____

_____

_____

_____

_____

_____

_____

_____

_____

Thought for the day
What do success and failure have in common? It seems that in this drama we call life these two concepts would be at opposite ends of the spectrum. What they have in common is simply this; neither one has the capacity to be permanent. Tough times come and go. Loves are found and lost. We have breathed life into hope only to see hope dashed on the rocks of life. We've rallied with success only to see times change and success flee. It would be in my best interest if I could let go of these old thoughts and simply be free to experience life as it is. My willingness to grow and change is not contingent on success or failure. My spiritual life is not dependent on success or failure. My ability to love is not defined by success or failure. I do not submit my life to the old standards and appraisals of success or failure. I seek freedom, faith and love. These are timeless God-given qualities that define themselves with no help or interpretation needed.

Meditation for the day
I replace the concept of success with 'benefit'. Are my actions beneficial to the people in my life? Are my thoughts positive and do my actions benefit me? I remove the concept of failure from my mind and life altogether. As I move away from the hard constraints of success and failure it is much easier for me to achieve my goals. My goal is to be beneficial to all.

Prayer for the day
I pray that once again I find new ways to define who I am and which path I wish to walk. I pray to remain flexible in thought and deed. I pray

to have the hard concepts of success and failure removed from my life so that I can be free to work for the benefit of all.

Mantra for the day
 Today I am beneficial. Today I am beneficial. Today I am beneficial.

Reflection for the day

_____

_____

_____

_____

_____

_____

_____

_____

_____

_____

_____

_____

_____

_____

Thought for the day

It seems that women are more comfortable in themselves than men. Women tend to embrace life while men tend to be in competition with self and others and fight in order to conquer life. If a woman sees a mountain she can enjoy its beauty without climbing it, a river without crossing it, a human being without the need to defeat it. Many men seek to win at all costs. When love finally humbles the male, he becomes willing to be open-minded. In this new thought he is able to learn peace and compassion. The efforts of an enlighten woman can make this transition smooth. When the man surrenders to the power and authority of the woman, he can be free from all the negatives that have driven him. Free to find a comfortable beauty wherever he looks, free to be at one with the universe. A man cannot learn these lessons from other men, he must learn from an enlightened woman if he truly seeks to be free.

Meditation for the day

Today I understand the distress that many men live with. I seek to be of use to willing males so that they can start their journey and transformation to peace and fulfillment. Never has the old saying 'surrender to win' had so much meaning. When a male gives up his hard fought masculine pride in favor of a female-led relationship, he indeed becomes a winner.

Prayer for the day

Today I pray to make my compassion visible and inviting. My hope is to bring peace to those I meet and the world in general. There is nothing or no one to fight only positive energy to be

shared. I pray to be an example of God's goodness
here on earth and helpful to all children of the
Divine. There is no competition in God's love.

Mantra for the day
  My peace and compassion will motivate
others. My peace and compassion will motivate
others. My peace and compassion will motivate
others.

Reflection for the day

_____

_____

_____

_____

_____

_____

_____

_____

_____

_____

_____

_____

_____

_____

Thought for the day

It appears that society today tries to impose a type of impersonalized victimization upon us. It is apparent that no one wants to take claim for the pain and the turmoil that they create in our lives. If we try to call about a bill or needing some type of help we are run around and around. We are routinely discounted as if we don't matter. This is how the world slowly seeks to disempower us and beat us into a state of blind compliance to their wishes. We push buttons on the phone endlessly only to be placed on hold for twenty minutes and then not helped at all. As frustrating as all of this is; there is one thing I know for sure. Impersonalized victimization or any other type of victimization can only be overcome with personal empowerment. As I grow, as I change, as I claim my power as queen, the chance of anyone imposing any type of negativity on me diminishes dramatically.

Meditation for the day

I review my past and see that my former feelings of being a victim were imposed on me with my consent. NO MORE. From this day forward I refuse to contemplate or participate in negativity. I find the responsible party and hold them accountable. It doesn't matter if it is the utility company, employer or romantic relationships. There is no more victimization in my life. There is no more quiet compliance to the wishes of malicious predators.

Prayer for the day

I pray for the strength to beat back the impersonal predators of the world. I stand my ground. I no longer simply succumb to the imposed pressures of the world. I am a goddess and a queen and I pray to always maintain my position of power and dignity when dealing with the evils of the world.

Mantra for the day
I will not accept unacceptable behaviors. I will not accept unacceptable behaviors. I will not accept unacceptable behaviors.

Reflection for the day

_____

_____

_____

_____

_____

_____

_____

_____

_____

_____

_____

_____

_____

_____

Thought for the day

Why do I question all? Sometimes I seek with the best of intent and sometimes with a heartless expression that causes failure in all. My goal as a woman should be to accept life as it is. Go with the flow, stop the fight, and surrender to the goodness that is always available. When a woman is enlightened she will cease the fight and begin to enjoy life. People come and people go. Situations change; sometimes to our liking sometimes not. The freedom of enlightenment is just that…freedom. This is the type of freedom that removes us from want, desire, and need; freedom to give from the heart and to accept what is given graciously. The men who serve me are there because I offer them the freedom to be who they are. The sisters in my circle are there because we seek the same freedom from the demands of life. When the harsh questions and judgments of reality fall by the wayside I will be free at last.

Meditation for the day

Everything just is. How simple is that? I have a good life because I have chosen to live a good life. Today, I realize that my head and my heart work in concert to liberate me from the daily grind that destroys many other people. I am strong because I am free.

Prayer for the day

I pray to rightly use my freedom and extend that same freedom to those deserving of my attention. Questions without answers are frustrating. I choose to live responsibly in the moment and embrace the love that is available. I pray for a spiritual liberation from this world, so that I too, may liberate those before me.

Mantra for the day

I am strong because I choose to be free. I am strong because I choose to be free. I am strong because I choose to be free.

Reflection for the day

_____

_____

_____

_____

_____

_____

_____

_____

_____

_____

_____

_____

_____

_____

Thought for the day

Have you ever thought, "Why me? Why now?" We can easily be drawn into self-pity. Most people experience this at one time or another. Depending on your self-image, these emotions can be experienced and then released without much effort. However, when a negative sense of self is what dominates, self-pity can spiral into 'what did I do to deserve this', 'maybe this is what I deserve', 'poor me'. We can change this with a little effort. I need to recognize the negative messages I tell myself and change them to positive. Write it down if needed. Make two columns; list the negative on the left and the new positive thoughts about yourself and your life on the right. Each time the negative pops in, tell yourself the positive. Do this as many times as you need. It takes practice to change the self-pitying mind-set many have developed. But we didn't learn to walk in one day, now did we?

Meditation for the day

Today my focus is on learning to practice changing the negative, self-pity into which I can easily fall. I believe I have that power to create that change. I just need to act on it consciously. My thoughts will flow to the positive life I want to create for myself and the positive attributes innately available.

Prayer for the day

I pray for wisdom and insight to my strengths. I ask for wisdom and humility to recognize those strengths and put them into practice in my life daily.

Mantra for the day
    Practice, practice, practice.

Reflection for the day

_____

_____

_____

_____

_____

_____

_____

_____

_____

_____

_____

_____

_____

_____

_____

_____

_____

_____

Thought for the day

If I choose to be a leader, I also need to accept the responsibilities of that role. First and foremost I need to do no harm. I do this by understanding the needs and taking into consideration the wants of all of those involved. The other greater and more satisfying part of good leadership is creating a safe and secure atmosphere that promotes success for all involved. When we create an environment that is conducive to growth, other people will feel secure enough to enter. Everyone will respond better and more effectively in an environment of love and compassion. I lead with love and compassion not by mandate.

Meditation for the day

I consider just what it is that I'm trying to achieve in my life, and ask myself how my enhanced success can benefit those who seek to please me. There are givers and receivers and while these roles, by necessity, constantly vacillate, I need to remain mindful that today I am primarily a receiver. By taking on a leadership role I create a positive environment for those who give to express themselves and therefore find personal fulfillment.

Prayer for the day

I pray for humility in my leadership role. I ask that I remain a compassionate leader and not a heartless dictator. I cannot be a leader if I have no followers. I ask for a full measure of compassion and an open heart to appropriately use the resources available to me for the benefit of all.

Mantra for the day

I lead with love and compassion. I lead with love and compassion. I lead with love and compassion.

Reflection for the day

_____

_____

_____

_____

_____

_____

_____

_____

_____

_____

_____

_____

_____

_____

_____

_____

_____

Thought for the day

Let's look at the different way in which men and women posses and apply their personal power. Men tend to horde power in an effort to prove worth and personal potency. Men don't like to share power. They are more inclined to use it to manipulate people to their advantage. Women posses their own brand of power; this frees them to take a totally different approach to its application. Women share the power that they have in an effort to motivate others. Gender seems to make a huge difference in the application of the same power. Males manipulate, women motivate. Which of these two approaches would seem most likely to benefit the greater number of people? As a people we can no longer work selfishly and expect long-term, positive results. To promote worthwhile change through the application of our power we must at all times look for and seize opportunities to be useful and beneficial to others.

Meditation for the day

I have felt the kindness of the world slipping away. Women cannot afford to pursue the path of males in an effort to be equal. We must claim our power and rise to our true potential as kind and loving representatives of our Creator. I am spiritually safe and protected; therefore, I can afford to work for the benefit of others. I am guided by faith not ruled by fear. The Power flows through me so that others may be helped, not exploited.

Prayer for the day

I pray to live my faith and therefore be free from the foolish, malignant application of power. I am the gift and I share the gift of my power and love for the benefit of all.

Mantra for the day
The Power is mine to share. The Power is mine to share. The Power is mine to share.

Reflection for the day

_____

_____

_____

_____

_____

_____

_____

_____

_____

_____

_____

_____

_____

_____

_____

_____

_____

Thought for the day

When I meet people with big, predatory personalities, I often feel they are trying to devalue me. This misappropriation of power is intended to give me cause to doubt myself and therefore lose faith in my own abilities. If I allow them get away with this devaluation, next they will try to impress me with their knowledge and convince me they have all of the answers I need. If I fall for this line of thinking, it is at this point, that I have abandoned my own faith in self and handed my personal power over to the malicious voices once again. Today I can see this sick game for what it is and I refuse to play. Today the people that come into my life to help me do not devalue me. These kind-hearted people quietly offer their resources to me for fun and for free. I need to be able to recognize the motives behind the people that I deal with. Good emotional choices are based on want, not need.

Meditation for the day

As I stay strong, the predators of the world will pass me by. I see that I may need to question myself from time to time, but I need never lose faith in myself or my abilities. When I lose faith in my abilities I create emotional need for fulfillment and I open the doors to the least desirable people. I will no longer open my heart to pain.

Prayer for the day

I pray for discernment in my interactions with others. I ask to continuously keep my spirit strong so my emotions will not be based on need. I cannot be useful to my Creator or others if I am emotionally needy. I am fulfilled and satisfied with my faith in God and myself.

Mantra for the day

Faith does not need. Faith does not need.
Faith does not need.

Reflection for the day

_____

_____

_____

_____

_____

_____

_____

_____

_____

_____

_____

_____

_____

_____

_____

_____

_____

Thought for the day

The use of my free will nearly destroyed me.
I did what I wanted, when I wanted, if I wanted. I
acted as if I were a selfish male. Today my
hardships have brought peace. They have also
brought the gift of enlightenment that I am all too
willing to share. I see that if I chose to interact with
a male I cannot in good conscious allow him the
same freedom that once nearly destroyed me. God
has given me the combined gifts of intelligence,
spiritual awareness and kindness. I will use these
gifts to guide the men in my life to a new and better
understanding of the joys to be found in meaningful
service.

Meditation for the day

I see how my service to God has brought my
freedom. I hope to bring this same awareness to
males. By keeping myself strong, by standing on
my spiritual principles and morals, men will
naturally be called to surrender themselves. I will
accept this as a beginning of their spiritual journey.
Goodness always triumphs over evil. I am
goodness. I will lead with firmness and fairness so
they too can be fulfilled.

Prayer for the day

I pray that God's goodness enables me to be
a good leader. I pray that I remain strong in my
spiritual beliefs. I pray that I can motivate the men
in my life to see that their true nature is one of
service to a loving, strong and spiritually motivated
woman.

Mantra for the day

God loves me, I am a leader, I am a guide. God loves me, I am a leader, I am a guide. God loves me, I am a leader, I am a guide.

Reflection for the day

_____

_____

_____

_____

_____

_____

_____

_____

_____

_____

_____

_____

_____

_____

_____

_____

_____

Thought for the day

Passive: not active, but acted upon, affected by outside forces.
Assertive: to affirm or state positively.
Aggressive: disposed to attack or encroach.

This should make our choices for life a little easier. I need to move away from my passive stance, and stop short of aggression. My passivity has brought me pain and my aggression has created pain for myself and others. Through prayer and the people in my life I have been better able to define myself, my wants and desires. Today, with illusion and doubt removed, I can assert myself with assurance. Gone are the days of turning to others for my worth. Gone are the days of emotional discord and fear that propelled me to be aggressive. I am peacefully at place in the middle of my emotions.

Meditation for the day

I carefully review my life for the errors I've made in the development of my character. I do not need to feel the power of a victim, nor am I inclined to feel the fear of the aggressor. I need to rightly center my life and emotions. I need to take a stand and firmly present my convictions. With a positive attitude and firm convictions, I can once again have hopeful expectations of myself and others.

Prayer for the day

I pray to rightly seek my place in life. I pray to move away from the burdens of the past and rise to my true station in life. I do not want to become what I see so distasteful in others. I want to be me,

centered, strong, assertive and assured. ME! As
defined by ME!

Mantra for the day

I am an enlightened woman; I have hopeful
expectations. I am an enlightened woman; I have
hopeful expectations. I am an enlightened woman;
I have hopeful expectations.

Reflection for the day

_____

_____

_____

_____

_____

_____

_____

_____

_____

_____

_____

_____

_____

Thought for the day

It has been said that honesty is the first page in the book of life. We think that if we tell the truth we are being honest. The truth is the truth and stands by itself. Honesty is the measure of our pursuit and movement toward the truth. Can I legitimately say that my motives have been pure in my dealings in life? Many times I have spoken the truth but skewed my progress toward honesty with less than desirable motives. For real progress to be made, I need to relieve myself of the unconscious defenses as well as the less than favorable motives I use to satisfy my selfish desires. If honesty is the first page in the book of life, elimination of self should be the preface. I cannot pursue a life of selfishness and expect to arrive at the truth. I need to purify my motives, pray for direction and move with honesty toward the truth.

Meditation for the day

Today I spend some time in thoughtful contemplation of the difference between truth and honesty. I realize that I need both of these qualities to establish and maintain the new direction of my life. I concentrate on the purity of my motives before I give life to their actions.

Prayer for the day

I pray for pure motives before I begin my honest walk toward the truth. I pray to have falsehoods and scandalous stimulus removed so my walk will be Divinely illuminated and genuinely rewarding for all.

Mantra for the day

Honesty must be pursued or falsehood will overtake us. Honesty must be pursued or falsehood will overtake us. Honesty must be pursued or falsehood will overtake us.

Reflection for the day

_____

_____

_____

_____

_____

_____

_____

_____

_____

_____

_____

_____

_____

_____

_____

_____

Thought for the day

He will never be any better than I expect
him to be. Here is a call to re-examine our
relationships. What type of expectations do I have
for the men in my life? Have I fully explained my
needs, wants, and desires? Have I taken the time to
allow a capable man into my life? We discipline
ourselves and we discipline our children in an effort
to create a more fulfilling life. Why would I be
unwilling to provide loving discipline for a man?
As the head of the house, it is my privilege to
provide growth opportunities for all in my home as
I see fit. With a joyous heart and a gentle spirit I
will set the pattern for our lives. I expect the men in
my life to work to please me and to aid in my
comfort. If a man cannot fully fathom the concept
that he is to be an asset in my life then he is indeed
a liability. If this is the case he either needs to grow
or go.

Meditation for the day

Have I given the men in my life the
information they need to grasp the growth
opportunities that I have availed them? It would be
a gross injustice to my God and my heart not to give
everyone the chance to be successful. A true queen
is always fair in her judgments, and does not easily
surrender her dreams for others without woe.

Prayer for the day

I pray to profoundly touch the men in my
life. I pray to encourage them to be more at peace
with themselves through their submission to loving
female authority. I pray to always use my powers
wisely to guide with love. I am the gift; I will teach
the men in my life how to ready themselves for me.

Mantra for the day

      I have expectations of goodness for those I love. I have expectations of goodness for those I love. I have expectations of goodness for those I love.

Reflection for the day

_____

_____

_____

_____

_____

_____

_____

_____

_____

_____

_____

_____

_____

_____

_____

_____

_____

_____

Thought for the day

Love and lust; how very nice when these two emotions come together. Unfortunately, they seem to cancel one another out. Often if we have one, then we can't have the other. Lust is probably responsible for more 'false love' and destroyed lives that anything else. When we do make the transition past lust to love, we sometimes lose the lust. The purpose of lust is to simply create the attraction and sustain our interest until we can find the love that we need to build a relationship on a more meaningful basis. I, too, was brought up with this erroneous fairy tale and have played a role in my own and other's destruction because I've demanded too much lust and given too little love. Lust is physical, love is spiritual. All we need to do is watch our bodies age to know that nothing physical will last. However, with our spirit and emotions, our ability to give and receive universal love is infinite.

Meditation for the day

I realize that lust is a transitional experience. I also realize that I have fallen victim to its call in the past with disastrous results. I do acknowledge the power and pleasure in lust, but from now on I will control it. Lust will become his burden to bear not mine. He desires, I am desired. The greater his need the greater my power!

Prayer for the day

I pray for discernment in the matters of lust and love. I pray to ever be mindful that I create the lust and I control the lust. Love is a free flow of all the goodness in the universe. I am always willing

to openly and freely share with other like-minded
people.

Mantra for the day
        The greater his need the greater my power.
The greater his need the greater my power. The
greater his need the greater my power.

Reflection for the day

_____

_____

_____

_____

_____

_____

_____

_____

_____

_____

_____

_____

_____

_____

_____

_____

Thought for the day
Often when women cry people think it's because they are confused and don't know what to do. They usually do know what to do and are crying out of frustration. The aggrieved are usually upset that their situation will not yield to more love, more understanding and more compassion. While these may well be considered traditional female qualities they are not readily applicable in this patriarchal society. Nobody wants to see a woman cry. Yet today mankind tries to force a woman to harden herself and comply with the heartless mandates of the current community. However, her tender spirit knows better. So she cries. She cries for the powerless the hungry and the neglected. She cries for the ignorant who refuse to yield to the coming of the new day. She cries for many and for all, but never herself; for she is strong. Strong enough to voice a tearful cry against the senseless hatred she is forced to live in.

Meditation for the day
My tears do not make me weak, they make others strong. My tears speak of injustice, frustration, and ignorance. My tears speak of the slow transition to female rule. My tears tell the story of many who have given up the noble fight in defeat. My tears also motivate me to work for and promote the change to matriarchy where peace and love will prevail.

Prayer for the day
I pray for the less fortunate. I pray for the sorrow bound and those with soul-sickness. I pray for all who stand in the way of women's enlightenment. I ask for a call to reason and the end

of violence, hunger, and war. I pray for a mass rising of women to take their rightful place as leaders in the home and in the world so that the peace of matriarchy may prevail.

Mantra for the day
       My tears are heard. My tears are heard. My tears are heard.

Reflection for the day

_____

_____

_____

_____

_____

_____

_____

_____

_____

_____

_____

_____

_____

_____

_____

Thought for the day

Today I count my blessings. I realize that I have moved from a fear based life to a faith based life. I also consider my ability to love and to receive love. I think we can always love; however, the inner turmoil we sometimes feel can restrict our ability to receive love. We should be, as God's agents, a vital part in the effort to keep the universal love moving. It flows from God to people, and my job is to take a little Divine love and pass on the rest. This I have learned over the years when the flow of love stops the sickness begins. Often in my past I would let fear stop the flow of love through me, and each time, invariably, I would become emotionally sick. If I am to forever grow in the love and power that is God-given then I need to share that love and properly use the power. The flow of my Higher Power through me is one of the primary goals in my life.

Meditation for the day

Today I look to the transition my life has undergone. My tumultuous fears have been replaced by a quiet faith. Faith in God and myself has opened the door for true love to enter my soul. I look to love and faith as a sure way out of the fears of my past and as the pathway to peace and eternal glory. Today I live peacefully and faithfully for I am engaged in the free flow of Universal love.

Prayer for the day

I pray to be grateful for the opportunity to share in and to promote the love that drives the universe. My part in the application of love is equal to anyone else's. We all are equal in the eyes of God for we all have an endless supply of Divine love, goodness, and power to share. I pray to be an effective conduit in the universal flow of love.

Mantra for the day

      Love in; love out. Love in; love out. Love in; love out.

Reflection for the day

_____

_____

_____

_____

_____

_____

_____

_____

_____

_____

_____

_____

_____

_____

Thought for the day

I remember the old sex education classes in school. They seemed to teach of the power of the unrestrained male virility and the reluctantly passive acceptance of this power by the female. A woman's sexuality was demeaned for her menstrual cycles, her inability to control contraception, her slow rise to orgasm, and worst of all her desire to enjoy the sex act. They should have taught about the superiority of woman physically and psychologically. Basic biology goes like this: men desire and woman is desired. Who then has the advantage? Throughout nature and the dating world it is the males that dance, sing, crow, and gobble in an attempt to attract a female. ALWAYS, from the least evolved to the highest thinking goddess it is the woman who decides which male is worthy of HER time.

Meditation for the day

I contemplate the natural superiority of the female. I look across nature and society to see just how things really work. I strip away the male lies of female fragility and frigidity. These lies are designed to 'level the playing field' and demoralize the female to make her easier to control. I see myself as God intended me to be; desirous and worthy! I claim my natural superiority as a woman.

Prayer for the day

I pray to graciously claim my female superiority as one would receive any other precious gift. Today I give thanks that God gave me the power. I am desired. I am in power. I am the gift.

Mantra for the day

Man desires; woman is desired, I have every advantage. Man desires; woman is desired, I have every advantage. Man desires; woman is desired, I have every advantage.

Reflection for the day

_____

_____

_____

_____

_____

_____

_____

_____

_____

_____

_____

_____

_____

_____

_____

_____

_____

Thought for the day

You must be the change you wish to see in the world.—Mahatma Ghandi.

Understanding the fear of change helps to overcome it. We fear change because the now is familiar, even if the now is not the most pleasant. If I change, will I like it, will I be able to accomplish what it is I have set out to do, will it be okay? Here is a little known secret to adopting change in your life: If you don't like it, or are not successful in it, or if it doesn't feel alright, you can change again! Many people look at change as permanent but it doesn't have to be.

Meditation for the day

Today I can change how I see things or change what I want to do or be. It is really that simple. If I don't like the outcome, I can change again. It is the only constant in life, things will change.

Prayer for the day

I pray for wisdom in making changes in my life. I ask to be blessed with the courage and grace to acclimate myself to changes around me. I am thankful for the opportunities given and the strength to move forward in my life.

Mantra for the day

     I need not fear change rather I embrace it with strength, wisdom and faith. I need not fear change rather I embrace it with strength, wisdom and faith.

Reflection for the day

_____

_____

_____

_____

_____

_____

_____

_____

_____

_____

_____

_____

_____

_____

Thought for the day

It is true that the past is probably the greatest of all learning opportunities. However, I have no desire to be tortured by the past. It's funny, but I never sit down and torture myself with those old mathematical times tables from school. Yet with emotions...I suppose that I'm looking for some type of resolution, but there is no resolution in pain; it either is or it isn't. Pain is simply pain; it has no vested interest in us. Unlike physical pain emotional pain never comes uninvited. I shall come to realize that once a lesson is learned I no longer need to revisit it. I will no longer view the past with a masochistic perspective. Today when I look back I see lessons learned and an endless amount of love, joy, and happiness to be cherished. I choose to learn from the pain and cherish the gifts of love that have been there as well. I keep gifts for they are precious.

Meditation for the day

I ask myself just what is my fascination with the acquisition of pain. Do I use it to validate my current actions? Do I use it to stifle or promote negativity? Or do I use it as it should be used; simply to balance my life and my emotions?

Prayer for the day

I ask the Creative Force for balance. I want to learn from my past not be subject to it. My painful past can be my pathway to peace if I learn to use it wisely. I pray to view the good as well of the bad and to learn the lessons that will make me a better and more joyous woman.

Mantra for the day

    My pathway is peace. My pathway is peace.
My pathway is peace.

Reflection for the day

_____

_____

_____

_____

_____

_____

_____

_____

_____

_____

_____

_____

_____

_____

_____

_____

Thought for the day

Women are the givers of life. This is an indisputable fact. In the birthing process men are only helpmates. The woman has the right to choose who is going to father the child and when and how this will happen. With this thought in mind, it seems evident that women should be the leaders in their relationships. It is apparent that the plan was for a woman to raise and mold the next generation with the help of a man. To whom did God trust the most precious of all gifts? Who was given the honor and privilege of giving birth and the ongoing responsibility for the health and the intellectual well-being of the next generation? In our own times, we can see that as more and more women reach enlightenment and claim their own personal power, family dynamics are changing. Whether a woman is in the workforce or a stay-at-home mom, she no longer is the helpless, powerless pawn of patriarchy. More and more women are claiming their spiritual right as head of the household.

Meditation for the day

In the past, males were hunters and gatherers. Today for many, their roles are still the same. Men provide material goods and emotional support to the woman thus enabling her to remain strong, helping her to provide and promote the next generation.

Prayer for the day

I pray to see the truth and the simplicity of the Creator's plan. Part of this plan is for me to manage family resources and distribute love and intellectual opportunities to those in my life. I ask that I be given the ongoing ability to live within the guidelines that the Creator has set. I ask for knowledge to see myself as a leader and strength to carry out the Creator's plan.

Mantra for the day
   I am living the plan. I am living the plan. I am living the plan.

Reflection for the day

_____

_____

_____

_____

_____

_____

_____

_____

_____

_____

_____

_____

_____

_____

_____

_____

Thought for the Day

A woman's heart tends to be people-centered and reality-based. She knows that the fate of the next generation rests on how well she conducts herself today. What do the children see as they watch their mother move through life? We know that they will learn what they are taught, so our everyday actions are tremendously important. We change, grow, and demonstrate the way we feel about ourselves everyday. Our heart and actions must reflect our family connection, values, and the love that we have to share. Our reality needs to show our own personal management and responsibilities well met. We should always carry ourselves with dignity and self-respect so that our children will know these qualities are available to them as well. My daily walk will reflect my love and strength of character.

Meditation for the Day

I allow my daily activities to reflect my care and concern for those in my life. I need to keep an eye to the future, but I must also realize that through my actions today I am building a better tomorrow for all of my loved ones. My reality is today and my future is born in my daily actions.

Prayer for the Day

I pray that I not be diverted by wishful thinking. I know there is no substitute for hard work. I have a good work ethic and a willingness to keep trying. I ask that my efforts to live a quality life are found to be satisfying to myself and others.

Mantra for the Day

     I am a positive example of a strong woman in action. I am a positive example of a strong woman in action. I am a positive example of a strong woman in action.

Reflection for the day

_____

_____

_____

_____

_____

_____

_____

_____

_____

_____

_____

_____

_____

_____

Thought for the day

We are led to believe men are strong and some are. However, here is a fact to ponder. Men get in the most trouble legally and morally in between the time that they leave the control of their mother and the time they come under the loving authority of their wives. In this period, usually late teens to mid twenties, men are often to be found running in packs, spending their time on sports, drinking to excess and other illicit endeavors. This is when men can be found 'playing the field' and learning to devalue women. 'Playing the field' almost makes wanton lascivious unrestrained selfish sexuality sound romantic. If a woman 'plays the field' she is not so well thought of. Once a relationship is formed with an enlightened woman, a man can look to her for strength and guidance. Once guidelines are set, he often settles down and meets his responsibilities.

Meditation for the day

I can now see where my efforts to lead men to peace can benefit all of society. It seems that many men simply refuse to grow up unless they are under the watchful eye of a well informed woman. A woman, fully knowledgeable of her strength, with a sincere desire to lovingly mold her man into a productive member of society can change the world for the better. I can be that woman!

Prayer for the day

I pray for the knowledge and ability to see my true worth as a queen. I ask for the perseverance to withstand the resistance of men and current social standards. I pray to wisely use my abilities to create a better, more socially and domestically aware partner.

Mantra for the day

I use my gifts to benefit society. I use my gifts to benefit society. I use my gifts to benefit society.

Reflection for the day

_____

_____

_____

_____

_____

_____

_____

_____

_____

_____

_____

_____

_____

_____

Thought for the day

Discipline! Oh, how I used to hate this word. I felt that I was always subject to someone's misguided attempts to control me. Discipline was always negative and usually punitively applied. Today, I find through my own self-imposed discipline I have created a powerful, contented woman. I am responsible for my well-being. My discipline propels my spiritual growth and allows for appropriate interaction with others. Discipline is no longer the evil unknown; it is the basis of a new and a productive life.

Meditation for the day

Once more, my life has been subjected to my erroneous perceptions. Discipline is my friend, not my enemy. I seek to find the will and strength to further discipline myself thus allowing my continued creative growth. I am no longer subject to others, I have the control. I am capable.

Prayer for the day

I pray that with the power of God and the sisterhood I continue to review the misperceptions of life that I once thought were principles. Just because it was shown to me does not make it real. I pray for an open mind and heart to allow further exploration and personal growth.

Mantra for the day

When I discipline myself, no one else needs to. When I discipline myself, no one else needs to. When I discipline myself, no one else needs to.

Reflection for the day

_____

_____

_____

_____

_____

_____

_____

_____

_____

_____

_____

_____

_____

_____

_____

_____

_____

Thought for the day

Discipline! Oh, how I love this word today. With my personal discipline being firmly entrenched as the basis of my new life, I have found a new self-assurance. I find that men are now drawn to my power and not empowered by my weakness. The predators have fled. Today, I take the time and energy to offer to males the discipline that is needed for their spiritual growth. Today I can rightly use my intelligence and sensuality to guide him to a life of usefulness. With my capable tutelage, I use that which motivates, allowing them to see the whole woman. I apply positive discipline so that they may grow as I have. It would be an injustice not to lead the less informed to a clearer way of thinking. As a goddess, I am strong, I am capable.

Meditation for the day

Today I reflect on the changes in the power dynamics in my relations. Today people seek to include me; they seek my opinion and guidance. I am strong! Today I look people in the eye, not at my feet. My head is up, my heart is strong and I am a guide and a goddess for others.

Prayer for the day

Today I pray for the ability to encourage others wisely. I ask that while my desires are being met I do not forget that the goal of working with others is enlightenment. I pray for the goodness of my heart to kindly guide me to create a new and more useful relationships.

Mantra for the day

It is female privilege and honor to guide. It is female privilege and honor to guide. It is female privilege and honor to guide.

Reflection for the day

_____

_____

_____

_____

_____

_____

_____

_____

_____

_____

_____

_____

_____

_____

_____

_____

_____

_____

_____

Thought for the day

My body is mine to control. I will take care
of my earthly home and see that its needs are met. I
will no longer abuse my home or let another abuse
it. My body brings me many pleasures. I will
honor my home with proper maintenance. The
combination of manicures, pedicures, bubble baths
proper exercise, diet and relaxation are no less that I
deserve. If I choose to share my body, it will be
treated as a temple. My home will be treated with
loving attention to my satisfaction. I will not be
bashful or shy in my directions on how to best meet
my needs. I am enough. If I choose to make a gift
of myself to another they must realize my pleasure
comes first and foremost. <u>I am the gift;</u> they need
not be concerned with their own selfish wants. As a
goddess I deserve worship.

Meditation for the day

I recognize my physical worth to myself and
others. I treat myself as a queen. As a gifted
woman, all others attend to the needs of the goddess
with reverence. No exceptions!

Prayer for the day

I pray for the proper attitude about myself.
My desire is that I both internalize and externalize
my strength, worth and beauty. As a woman I am
the greatest of God's creations. I have respect for
the work of my Creator and will demand respect
from all others fortunate enough to come before me.

Mantra for the day

I treat my earthly home respectfully. I treat
my earthly home respectfully. I treat my earthly
home respectfully.

Reflection for the day

_____

_____

_____

_____

_____

_____

_____

_____

_____

_____

_____

_____

_____

_____

_____

_____

_____

Thought for the day

How very nice it is to be me! I do have my troubles and uncertainties, but I have been blessed with a wonderful, kind heart and an endless abundance of faith. I have the intelligence to question the information of the past, and to define a new life for myself and those around me. I cannot get where I want to go on yesterday's insight and information. I must constantly seek new enlightenment because I have a new, jubilant life through change. What a wondrous joyous experience to fully use my gifts as a woman. Today I can fully recognize my worth and unselfishly share my goodness with those fortunate people I meet. When my goodness comes from God, it is real and can not be defiled. I walk with Grace and an open, outreached hand for those still to come.

Meditation for the day

Today I meditate on how best to serve my God and help others. My gifts are many and a pleasure to share. I renounce the selfishness of this world and create opportunities to infuse the world with goodness. I cannot give away goodness faster than God gives it back.

Prayer for the day

I pray to be a helpful steward of the goodness that has been Divinely given to me. I ask to change the world. I know I am fortified with the Power. My goal is Love. Love changes the world, for others as well as for myself.

Mantra for the day

I change the world through love. I change
the world through love. I change the world through
love.

Reflection for the day

_____

_____

_____

_____

_____

_____

_____

_____

_____

_____

_____

_____

_____

_____

_____

_____

_____

_____

Thought for the day

Pain and penance: two of my old friends. It seems that I've spent way too much time with these two. We all have an adequate supply of pain in our lives. Sometimes though, we seek out a little extra pain that we can always find laying around and claim that discomfort as ours as well. I've measured my worth by the sorrow that I've gained. I've lived the life of a victim. I have both held, and irresponsibly shared my unwarranted sadness. I've used both my ability to withstand pain and my ability to pay penance as ways to validate myself. My long-suffering can become a very unnecessary and laborious lifestyle. The burden of self-inflicted penance has driven me to the edge of self-destruction many times. My suffering does not define me. Self-authentication through pain is not congruent with the love of God.

Meditation for the day

I recognize my past need to collect pain and suffering, then reflect on the troubles these actions have brought me. If it isn't love, it isn't God given. God ONLY deals in love. I need to refocus my energies in the proper direction. I leave the collection of torment and its price to someone better qualified to handle these demons. My sole focus is on the collection and manifestation of love. I seek light and I seek love. I am a woman of love.

Prayer for the day

I pray to move away from the collection of sorrow in my life. I ask to responsibly deal with my own issues. I do not take on discomfort that is not rightfully mine. My God will show me the way to love. I pray to walk with my Creator in the light of love and to be a beacon of Divine light for all.

Mantra for the day

My validation is in the love and light of God. My validation is in the love and light of God. My validation is in the love and light of God.

Reflection for the day

_____

_____

_____

_____

_____

_____

_____

_____

_____

_____

_____

_____

_____

_____

_____

_____

_____

Thought for the day

Courage is defined as a quality of mind or temperament that enables one to stand fast in the face of opposition, hardship or danger. Do mind and temperament equal spirit? I believe so. Courage evolves from the spirit although both are sometimes used synonymously. Courage can be described as fear that has said its prayers. We need a healthy dose of courage and humility to face many of the struggles of life: being a single mother, developing and running a business, being a compassionate friend and lover, remaining strong and riveted toward our ultimate goals in life. As superior women we are offered much diversity and opportunities to participate and contribute to the world. It is imperative that we remember this and find the courage to act.

Meditation for the day

I look to past instances wherein I needed a courage greater than I dreamed of possessing. I reflect on how to best use this new power to further our goals as women and to create a more developed mindset for all. As I am dauntless in my pursuit of feminine growth, my concentration remains on ways to increase love and personal integrity for the enlightened women of the day.

Prayer for the day

Today I ask for knowledge of mind, evenness of temperament and determination of spirit. I cast my doubts and cares upon the shoulders of Our Creator and walk upright with a strong and wise heart.

Mantra for the day

I have a determination of spirit known as courage. I have a determination of spirit known as courage.

Reflection for the day

_____

_____

_____

_____

_____

_____

_____

_____

_____

_____

_____

_____

_____

_____

_____

_____

Thought for the day

As women, we need not only to recognize our potential, but to nourish its growth in a most positive direction. We are strong and courageous, yet flexible and compassionate. These gifts, so freely given us by our Maker, reflect the goodness of our soul. As we start each day we embrace our strength, the collective strength of womankind. Know that we are here for each other, beholding and supporting our sisters in thought and deed. Let us all be proud by our actions.

Meditation for the day

Today, I focus on the power found in numbers. If I falter, I think to the mother staying awake with a sick child or the scientist striving for a cure; the teacher working to help the children understand or the politician building a stronger world, the daughter holding her ailing mother's hand. I gain strength from the wondrous miracle that is woman. The gift I am, we all are.

Prayer for the day

I pray to honor the women in my life, in my sphere, in our world through the gifts of strength, courage, and love. I pray to set the example for my daughters, your daughters.

Mantra for the day

I am an honorable women bonded with other women in strength and courage. I am an honorable woman, bonded with other women in strength and courage.

Reflection for the day

_____

_____

_____

_____

_____

_____

_____

_____

_____

_____

_____

_____

_____

_____

Thought for the day

I am not my body and I will not be restrained by it. How wonderful it is to be young and have the strength of body and a character that has not yet been fully tested. As our body ages and our physical limitations mount we rely more and more on our mental faculties. The obstacles that were once overcome with might now are finessed with mental and emotional energies. I find a freedom and liberation from my body. I like knowing that I am NOT who other people perceive me to be based on my physical characteristics. Although there may be things I dislike about my body, my spirit allows me to find wonderful things to love about me. I am so very, very much more than I appear to be. I need to move beyond what I view as physical limitations and find the real me. I embrace the character, and strength that is hiding within yearning to be fully born once more.

Meditation for the day

My mother gave birth to my body only once, but I can give myself birth any time I choose. Born again, rebirth, renewal, call it what you will; it is mine to claim. When faced with the emotional pain of this life I am simply be reborn once again. It sounds strange but it is just like turning the page. I am free from physical and emotional limitations when I choose to be reborn.

Prayer for the day

If I can't get my body and soul united, I choose my soul. One day I will leave this old body behind, but my soul is mine to keep, so it is where my energies go. I ask the Spirit for continuous direction in the nourishment of the real me. I can always be at peace with the REAL me; my spirit, my soul!

Mantra for the day

I am not my body. I am not my body. I am not my body.

Reflection for the day

_____

_____

_____

_____

_____

_____

_____

_____

_____

_____

_____

_____

_____

_____

_____

_____

Thought for the Day

The only way I can change what I think is by changing what I think. Simple, but not easy. In order for me to take on new ideas, I need to cast off the old ones. I cannot become a new woman based on my former thoughts and beliefs. If I want a new life, I need to create a new woman. We often hear feminists referred to as liberated. Liberated from what? Liberated from the past; free to take on new ideas free to create and stand on new belief systems, liberated from our former way of thinking. Once I can distance myself from the past, then I need to carefully choose my new belief system and set it into action. I can be anyone I want to be. I can interact with the world and its people just as I choose. This is liberation and this is freedom. It is mine to claim. This is the pathway to the new woman I choose to be.

Meditation for the Day

I consider what ties me to my former beliefs. Are these restraining beliefs genuinely mine or were they foisted on me by others? Do I need them to feel safe, limited and therefore secure? Can I rightly see which ideas I need to cast off and exchange for those which will better suit the new woman that I am?

Prayer for the Day

Oh Great Creator of all, I come to You and ask for freedom from my past. I ask that You grant me strength as I start a new journey into self-discovery and personal fulfillment. It is through Your knowledge, strength and peace that I grow.

Mantra for the Day

Freedom is mine to claim. Freedom is mine to claim. Freedom is mine to claim.

Reflection for the day

_____

_____

_____

_____

_____

_____

_____

_____

_____

_____

_____

_____

_____

_____

_____

_____

_____

Thought for the day

I need to share my thoughts and ideas with other women. There is much strength in the power of sisterhood. I view other women as helpers and educators, not as competition. Women must stand united for the good of the world. The division, violence, and competition in which we have been forced to live and raise children must be put to rest. Man has tried for centuries to dominate the world and the women in it. He has not and will never succeed. It's not so much a war of the sexes as a war between good and evil. Goodness will always prevail. Now that the world is becoming more female-focused and women are rising to political power, we can begin to expect rapid changes.

Meditation for the Day

Today I look for the strength to make a difference in the world. I take a stand for peace and kindness. Far too many times I have let malicious statements and behaviors of others pass me by without comment. I can remain calm and in control. Yet, I can still voice concerns regarding my views of society. As an enlightened woman I have a responsibility to add my voice to the chorus of women working for peaceful change and the betterment of society.

Prayer for the Day

I ask to be united with other like-minded, intelligent women of change. Unless I use my voice, I am not heard. I pray to rightly use my talents to work to change the world. I also seek to inspire others to rise to the cause of peace.

Mantra for the Day

Together we are strong. Together we are strong. Together we are strong.

Reflection for the day

_____

_____

_____

_____

_____

_____

_____

_____

_____

_____

_____

_____

_____

_____

_____

_____

_____

_____

Thought for the day

I was always told that in the rough waters of life that I needed faith. However, no one ever told me how to find it. Hope is not faith, belief is not faith and desire is not faith; so what is faith and how do I find it? I cannot have faith in anything that I've never used. Here is a recipe that I like: belief + decision + action = faith. First, I must come to believe differently if I am to change. Secondly, I must make a solid decision to change. Finally, of course (and this can be the hard part), I must apply whatever actions are needed to promote the desired change. Faith is the result of actions taken. I had no real faith in God until I applied this simple recipe. I had no faith in myself or my power because I had never believed in me or taken any actions to use my power. Today the combination of faith in God, faith in myself, and faith in my personal power has given me a new and fulfilling life; a life of faith that I can believe in because I have used it.

Meditation for the day

My faith is strong because I have taken positive actions to serve my God and to promote myself and others. I have seen and felt the Power of the universe; this Power is mine to use as well. I can have faith in many things and many people. I do not limit my faith or question the faith of others. I can learn from others' beliefs and actions.

Prayer for the day

I pray to ever increase my faith through my actions. Faith is an action word; I must take action if I wish to see results. Faith doesn't come to me, I must move ever closer to it.

Mantra for the day

     I am willing to work for my faith. I am willing to work for my faith. I am willing to work for my faith.

Reflection for the day

_____

_____

_____

_____

_____

_____

_____

_____

_____

_____

_____

_____

_____

_____

_____

_____

_____

_____

Thought for the day

It's true, I used to be a bitch; but no more. I used *my will* and *my power* to promote myself at the expense of others. Today I can look back over these days with amused disbelief. How was I able to believe that negative energy could promote positive change? Today I realize that I *AM* a goddess. I believe my positive energy can change the world for the better. The misuse of negative energy made me a bitch. The appropriate use of positive energy makes me a queen!

Meditation for the day

I focus on the positive energy that flows from God and through me. I consult with my Creator on how best to promote Spiritual love and learn to value myself as I am valued.

Prayer for the day

I pray that I can appropriately learn to use the love and power of God in my life. My heart will lighten, my smile will brighten. People will be drawn to me as an enlightened and powerful woman.

I am a queen, I am a goddess, and God loves me. I am a queen, I am a goddess and God loves me. I am a queen, I am a goddess and God loves me.

Reflection for the day

_____

_____

_____

_____

_____

_____

_____

_____

_____

_____

_____

_____

_____

_____

_____

Thought for the day

Who is your hero? People often see heroism as synonymous with bravery. Characteristics of a hero can be listed as courage, strength, skill, expertise, and intelligence. A hero is generous, loving, shows affection, is honest and a risk-taker. Growing up our heroes were Superman, Batman, the cop on the beat, the astronaut, the president. However, most of these heroes were men. There is nothing wrong with having a man for a hero, but there are many women described by these characteristics that are omitted solely because they are women. When you think of yourself, how many of these attributes describe you? We overlook the most obvious out of fear of being conceited, afraid to act as if we may be better than the roles allotted to us by a male dominated society. Be a hero to the young women around you, be your own hero.

Meditation for the day

Today I reflect on the qualities I possess as a hero. I look to the female heroes in my life: my mother struggling to make ends meet and take care of a sick father, my teacher striving to reach young minds and enrich them, my friend struggling through her divorce while working to support her children. I see in them the qualities that make them a hero to me and focus on growing the attributes of character that make me a hero as well.

Prayer for the day

I request direction in lending the qualities so freely given to other women in my life. I ask for humility and a generous spirit to share these gifts.

Mantra for the day

  I am a hero for myself and others. I am a hero for myself and others. I am a hero for myself and others.

Reflection for the day

_____

_____

_____

_____

_____

_____

_____

_____

_____

_____

_____

_____

_____

_____

_____

_____

_____

_____

Thought for the day

First God created man. Then with considerable thought and effort his greatest creation, WOMAN was born. Part of her greatness comes from what she doesn't have. She doesn't have a need to selfishly dominate for the sake of power and ego. She doesn't need to control with fear. She doesn't need to take to receive and validate herself. She knows that her candle does not burn brighter when she blows out another's. I am a woman; I am God's greatest creation. I WILL act like it and set an example for my sisters and set the standard for males to strive for.

Meditation for the day

Today I see myself as I really am; the greatest of all creations. I thank my God for taking time to perfect me and for giving me the strength to meet Divine standards. I am love, I am kindness, and I am a leader and a grateful servant. Today I serve my God, support my sisters, and am a leader of men. This I can do for I have been bestowed with greatness.

Prayer for the day

I pray that I do not squander the greatness that has been bestowed upon me. Today I realize that God's gifts are given to me to rightly use for the benefit of others. I pray that I continue to be a kind supporter and a firm leader.

Mantra for the day

I live at peace with God's greatest creation. I live at peace with God's greatest creation. I live at peace with God's greatest creation.

Reflection for the day

_____

_____

_____

_____

_____

_____

_____

_____

_____

_____

_____

_____

_____

_____

_____

_____

_____

_____

Thought for the day

There really are good men out there that want to please. Unfortunately no one has ever taught them how. Fear, ego, self-centeredness, and ignorance all conspire to make them less than useful to an enlightened woman. One of the best things a woman can do for a man is to be firm in her beliefs and convictions. She need not waver in her expectations. Another helpful tool is real, honest communications. Make clear statements and directives. Once a man makes the commitment to stay with you, give him the information he needs to be successful. Allow him to feel good about the joy he brings you and the pleasure he provides. Men like to feel useful and victorious. If he can succeed in bringing you pleasure on your terms and feel that through his actions he has earned a place in your life, he will feel better and more secure. These positive feelings and emotions can then be shared with you.

Meditation for the day

I am firm and fair in my treatment of others. I give them the information that they need to be successful and useful. I must remember they have sought me out. They have been attracted by my power and strong presence. They view me as wise and superior, and for once they are right! Clear statements of my expectations, backed by a willingness to help them succeed will benefit all. Taking the time to enlighten men to be more useful is never wasted energy.

Prayer for the day

I pray that my efforts to enlighten men make them more content with themselves and more useful to women. All women need to enhance the lives of men so the world can become a better, more pleasurable female-centered place.

Mantra for the day
      My efforts to educate are not in vain. My efforts to educate are not in vain. My efforts to educate are not in vain.

Reflection for the day

_____

_____

_____

_____

_____

_____

_____

_____

_____

_____

_____

_____

_____

_____

_____

_____

Thought for the day

Bad boy, bad boy! Here is a painful little diversion either we've fallen into or some of our friends have. There are several things going on here. One is that we are allowed to live vicariously. We are emotionally (hopefully not physically) connected to the excitement of bad choice and bad behavior. Find a bad boy and you let him live your dreams of danger and excitement. The other is the erroneous exercise of my power and control. 'He'll quit for me.' 'He wouldn't quit for them, but he will for me.' Therefore I am wonderful! Needless to say this application of our time, talent and power to a no-win situation is a waste of energy. Bad boys are emotionally and financially draining. They rarely change at depth and the woman finds herself shattered in his wake as he glides effortlessly on to the next woman looking for a challenge. Bad boys are users.

Meditation for the day

I search myself to find what calls me to such a negative situation. What is it inside of me that is drawn to change and conquer the hopelessly ignorant? There are plenty of good, healthy, happy men out there that long for true application of my character. I seek to satisfy my needs with the help of a loving Spirit so I won't fall into a no-win, at-any-cost type of relationship.

Prayer for the day

I pray to fight the battles within myself with the help of a loving God and not a mean-spirited boy. The only thing in this life worth fighting for is love; and we've already established the universe has

an endless supply of it available to me if only I
seek. I have no need for conflict.

Mantra for the day
      Negativity is a waste of my energy.
Negativity is a waste of my energy. Negativity is a
waste of my energy.

Reflection for the day

_____

_____

_____

_____

_____

_____

_____

_____

_____

_____

_____

_____

_____

_____

_____

Thought for the day

Happiness is an illusion. It seems that everywhere we turn people are trying and dying to be happy. The problem with happiness is that its only true claim to fame is that it is simply the culmination of my selfish desires. Something either within or without must meet my standards for me to be happy. Joy, on the other hand, is a solitary endeavor. My joy is in response to the universal free flow of love that is always available to everyone. Joy can be maintained, expanded and shared without any input from anyone. My joy is contingent on my relationship with my Creator. My joy is not contingent upon my selfish desires or the people in my life. We are all capable of joy. We should pursue, enhance and share our joy as a demonstration of a loving Spirit working through our heart.

Meditation for the day

I contemplate the differences between joy and happiness. Upon reflection, surely I come to the conclusion that a life based on the pursuit of happiness is fantasy; whereas the manufacture and distribution of joy can be an ongoing reality that cannot be abused. Happiness is conditional on others; joy stands alone willing to serve.

Prayer for the day

I pray to leave my self-based happiness behind in favor of the ongoing joy that will benefit all. My joy is a gift that can and will enhance the well-being of everyone I meet. I pray to share my joy, my God with all.

Mantra for the day
    I am joy. I am joy. I am joy.

Reflection for the day

_____

_____

_____

_____

_____

_____

_____

_____

_____

_____

_____

_____

_____

_____

_____

_____

_____

_____

Thought for the day

It has been said that there is one prayer that is always answered. That prayer is to simply ask to be willing to be willing. How many times have I needed to change, or wanted to change or even hoped to change without success? I have found myself seized with rebellion against the very changes that I most desire; positive changes that will benefit everyone that I love. I usually stay stuck on the backside of the line of contempt until a flurry of emotions motivates me to ask for and receive the willingness that I need to promote change. My willingness is one of the key elements that enable me to evolve. Whether I petition God or dig deep within, I can always find the little spark that I need to ignite a new plan of action.

Meditation for the day

I realize that resistance is futile. My new spiritual and emotional life will propel me to further my growth through willingness that is available to me by asking. Change is a process not an event. I need to seek willingness to promote the goals that I have set for myself.

Prayer for the day

I pray to be willing to be willing. I ask my God to help me be proactive in my decisions. I readily enhance my growth if I don't get stalled in the stubborn, self-imposed resistance that robs me of valuable time and energy. I am quick to ask for the Divine help that I need. I pray for positive action to promote positive change.

Mantra for the day

I am willing to be willing. I am willing to
be willing. I am willing to be willing.

Reflection for the day

_____

_____

_____

_____

_____

_____

_____

_____

_____

_____

_____

_____

_____

_____

_____

_____

_____

_____

Thought for the day

In my daily dealings with people I must not be judgmental. How often do I cast people or events as being 'good' or 'bad'? These people just simply believe differently from me. They do have a right to pursue their lives and express their opinions. Today I realize that it is my judgments blaring and veiled that have continuously thwarted my efforts at growth. Each of these infected determinations is of equal value. Whether they are outrageous or subconscious my judgments keep me blind to the truth. How often have I had to back-track, and work through my erroneous thinking only to arrive at the very point that I had departed my original journey? My judgments are self-defeating and hurtful.

Meditation for the day

Today I reflect back on my life and the role that my malicious use of judgment has played. Often I have used my condemnation of others and their beliefs to build a false sense of security for myself. In the past I have used character assassination to improve my opinion of myself. Today I seek to truly better myself though my ongoing spiritual development. Forevermore my personal growth will be dependent on love not turmoil and malice.

Prayer for the day

I pray to be open-minded enough to cheerfully grant others the same discretion that I seek for myself. If I want to enjoy the fruits of freedom I must sow the seeds of freedom. These seeds are found in the unselfishness of an open-mind, and a pure and thoughtful heart. These purified seeds of freedom are mine to cast.

Mantra for the day

I cheerfully grant the liberty I seek for myself to others. I cheerfully grant the liberty I seek for myself to others. I cheerfully grant the liberty I seek for myself to others.

Reflection for the day

_____

_____

_____

_____

_____

_____

_____

_____

_____

_____

_____

_____

_____

_____

_____

Thought for the day

What would a man gain by submitting to me? The best answer is simply this; balance. Many men are not raised in a balanced state. Far too many males are raised to exist in an unemotional state of perceived power and control. Unlike women, men are raised with far fewer emotional freedoms and options. Their social structure is much narrower and without the liberties of self-expression that many women take for granted. Much like we, as women, are trying to grow into a more assertive role to achieve balance many men need to yield to the power of an enlightened woman. This will give them the opportunity to gain a sense of balance. Most men are raised to defer to and respect women, but during adolescence and the male socialization process many men move away from their childhood teachings and pursue a lifestyle of self-importance and grandiosity. When they are properly encouraged to abandon their previous teachings and work through their fears of vulnerability and subjection, an enlightened male can find peace and comfort at last. He is able to lay down the warrior's shield that he uses to resist emotional closeness and empathy. At this point the male can then receive the rewards that we enjoy as we break the archaic societal bonds that have limited our growth as well. Freedom will benefit all!

Meditation for the day

Today I realize that by taking a leadership role in my relationships I am giving the gift of freedom. Just as I seek my strength and balance in a leadership role, he will find his strength and balance in a contributory role. Today I seek to

promote the best for everyone. I want those I love
to be free and I'm willing to work for their freedom.

Prayer for the day

     I pray to use my newfound strength and
power as a leader to further enhance my personal
relationships. I pray for kindness and direction to
clear the path for growth. I do not want those I love
to struggle for as long my sisters have. I encourage
loving surrender to promote emotional health,
freedom and balance.

Mantra for the day

     I work for those that I love. I work for those
that I love. I work for those that I love.

Reflection for the day

_____

_____

_____

_____

_____

_____

_____

_____

_____

_____

Thought for the day

The decisions that I make today may well not suit my future plans. It is nice to believe that I am on one long, smooth life path headed for endless amounts of earthly reward and heavenly bliss. However, I need only look back to see that the plans I made yesterday do not always fit today. This is as it should be. There is no need to be discouraged because my life has taken many paths. I need to celebrate my willingness to change with the times. It is important to always remember to stay flexible in my beliefs and actions. I am not be dismayed by the destination, or lack thereof, for my journey is always fruitful and sustaining. This journey is what this life is about, no more and no less. The people I meet, the pleasure that I feel, my own personal empowerment is my life. People come and go, pleasures change from moment to moment. Old loves fade and what I once saw as excitement now seems trite. I need to make plans but not plan the outcomes. I enjoy my life as it is today!

Meditation for the day

Focus and future are not necessarily synonymous. My thoughts change, my feelings change, and my future changes. It's in my best interest if I can learn to make my plans yet plan on the vicissitudes of life. Why would I need to go anywhere when I am here? They call this moment the present because it is God's gift to us. I will seek to graciously receive it and be content in this day.

Prayer for the day

I ask my God to bless me with the gratitude that this day is capable of bringing. I pray to make peace with the man-made concept of time and realize that I will face many changes on my journey to eternity.

Mantra for the day
My beliefs and actions will remain flexible. My beliefs and actions will remain flexible. My beliefs and actions will remain flexible.

Reflection for the day

_____

_____

_____

_____

_____

_____

_____

_____

_____

_____

_____

_____

_____

_____

_____

_____

Thought for the day

I am a gift, not a prize. I am not an item to be fought for or bartered for. The ego-driven ways of unenlightened men will not sway me. I am the gift. I decide who I bless with my smile or my presence. A prize is the result of a competition won. So many times, once this prize is acquired it is placed upon a shelf to be neglected like any other trophy. I have no desire to have my life limited for the glorification of a man's ego. I have important things to do, people to help, and my own successes to claim. I'm far too intelligent to get caught up in these juvenile games. Today I realize that men that try to entangle me are actually trying to impress themselves or their friends. While this behavior can be somewhat amusing to watch, I realize that an authentic man will set his life's goal to be helpful and pleasing to me. Heartfelt adoration and dedicated effort may catch my eye. A goddess is not to be neglected or put on a shelf.

Meditation for the day

I reflect on the dating/marriage games and how inadequate they are to building a healthy relationship. I see that this system was designed to benefit men not women. My former ways of thinking brought the same old sad results. My new way of thinking as an enlightened woman will bring an entirely different and more satisfying life. I am exalted and adored; this is no less than I deserve.

Prayer for the day

I pray to continuously work to enhance my new status in life. I offer myself to my God for guidance in my continued personal growth. I pray to graciously receive heartfelt service.

Mantra for the day

I am a gift to be given not a prize to be won. I am a gift to be given not a prize to be won. I am a gift to be given not a prize to be won.

Reflection for the day

_____

_____

_____

_____

_____

_____

_____

_____

_____

_____

_____

_____

_____

_____

_____

_____

_____

Thought for the day

Becoming empowered means we take responsibility for our own choices and our lives. Many of us were disempowered by relationships, shame, the perception we have of our lives, lack of altruistic purpose or many other demons that seem to erode our sense of self. Or it may be that sense didn't develop properly to begin with due to these factors and the effect on us while growing. As we develop a new sense of personal strength, we need to begin taking responsibility for our lives: our finances, our security, our direction, our feelings and our self-image. The magic to this is that as we begin doing these things, our positive self-image grows and blossoms. We no longer "have to have" this person, this thing, this place to be secure in who we are. Let go of the blanket, Linus! Everything will work out. It will do so at a level that allows me an inner pride and a sense of self that will not be shaken by outer circumstances or malicious people.

Meditation for the day

My focus for the day is growing myself through personal strength and satisfaction with who I am and where I am heading. I am planning the ways in which I am rebuilding my sense of self and strengthening my empowerment.

Prayer for the day

I continue to ask for strength and guidance in the life I am building. Help me to remain humble in my endeavors and always willing to reach out to other women with the same needs.

Mantra for the day

I am focused on growing my empowerment.
I am focused on growing my empowerment. I am
focused on growing my empowerment.

Reflection for the day

_____

_____

_____

_____

_____

_____

_____

_____

_____

_____

_____

_____

_____

_____

_____

_____

_____

Thought for the day

Each day I have choices. I can choose to be trusting, faithful and hopeful. When I make these choices I experience serenity, peace and love. My life mirrors my spiritual condition. When I am trusting in my God, I am confident. When my faith is strong, I am secure. When my hope is focused on positive outcomes, my belief in humanity is strong. The strength I have been gifted with permeates my being. With the guidance of the Spirit, I am whole and possess courage that allows me to face the daily fear of life and death without shuddering, but with a quiet acceptance that "it is well with my soul."

Meditation for the day

Today I focus on the powerful gift supplied. I will use it wisely and refuse to diminish it through unhealthy choices. I will banish fear and frailty and, as always, depend on my God to guide and strengthen my spirit.

Prayer for the day

I pray for the wisdom to use my gifts to honor my Creator. I pray for an ongoing alliance with the Spirit to bestow goodness and share the gifts so freely given. I pray to cherish the hope, nourish the faith, and build upon the trust that the Spirit and I have cultivated.

Mantra for the day

I am filled with trust, faith and hope. My actions will reflect these truths daily. I am filled with trust, faith and hope. My actions will reflect these truths daily.

Reflection for the day

_____

_____

_____

_____

_____

_____

_____

_____

_____

_____

_____

_____

_____

_____

_____

Thought for the day

Training the male! When I asked my friends to read these writings many exclaimed; oh no! That's too harsh. Well, it's not if we think about it. I take on new ideas. I follow up with actions. Then I either endorse or reject the results based on the positive or negatives found. I call this change. This is how we all change and grow. It is basic behavior modification principles. So if my 'training techniques' are good enough for me; why would they not also be good enough for the people with whom I choose to spend my time? Men and women are different and we stay different unless we make a huge effort to come together for anything other than sex. He needs to meet my expectations for I choose not to abandon my emotions. I choose to care more about people and promoting success than sports. I choose to go through this life with a warm and satisfied heart that is always willing to share. If we are to come together he must succumb to my standards for I will not lower myself to his!

Meditation for the day

I love men, but I must remain mindful that their archaic, Neanderthal principles will not be applicable in the new world we as women are creating. Women are more fully evolved and developed than men. If I choose to love a man, can I in good conscious allow him to falter and fall behind?

Prayer for the day

I give thanks to my Creator for allowing me to be born and live as a female. I also graciously give thanks to live in a time when female enlightenment and rule is *the* emerging societal attitude.

Mantra for the day
It's good to be queen! It's very good to be queen. It's great to be queen!

Reflection for the day

_____

_____

_____

_____

_____

_____

_____

_____

_____

_____

_____

_____

_____

_____

_____

Thought for the day

How often have I substituted control for love? In the past, I have been subject to and erroneously applied control in the name of love. Probably the best way to distinguish between these two is to be sure of our motives and our spiritual base. There is a fine line between exercising discipline and exerting control. The people in my life that choose to support me look to me for discipline and direction not control. This development of personal discipline is a natural expression of my power and a necessary element that will enable them to find their own personal power. The systematization that I apply to myself and others creates a comfortable structure for everyone to live within. We all need order in our lives to feel comfortable enough to seek to expand our horizons.

Meditation for the day

I reflect on how much better I feel when I seek to discipline rather than to control. There is an old saying that goes like this: he who is convinced against his will is of the same opinion still. As a woman of kindness and substance, one of my goals is to pave the way for positive change for others. When I set an example of a disciplined life, those who seek me out become convinced that they too can improve their lives.

Prayer for the Day

I ask in all sincerity for the gift of discernment in the application of the powers with which I have been blessed. I ask for kindness of heart, and purity character so I can positively influence those who rely on me.

Mantra for the day

     I am the gift of change. I am the gift of change. I am the gift of change.

Reflection for the day

_____

_____

_____

_____

_____

_____

_____

_____

_____

_____

_____

_____

_____

_____

_____

_____

Thought for the Day

When a man uses his resources to get his way, many are impressed. If he uses his finances or his body to manipulate others, he is held in high esteem. However, if a woman uses her attributes to obtain her desires, she is not so well thought of. Once more, we see a double standard that must be destroyed. Men fear women for their sensuality, so they seek to devalue them as people for using their natural attributes. In truth men envy women and stand in awe of their power and glory. I am a woman on the search for personal freedom and liberation from the restraints of society, and I will use my resources to my advantage. If I choose to honor a man with my presence, I can rightfully expect his full attention and devotion to my desires. I will no longer restrain or devalue myself for the protection of the male ego. My resources and power are mine to use to my advantage.

Meditation for the day

I wonder why I've spent so long being a 'good girl'. Why have I wasted my time trying to protect the people that have so often sought to use me to their advantage? What has kept me from freely using all of my resources? There is no one going to give me permission to grow or do the work for me. The future is mine, and I will make a conscious decision to seek my worth and to work for my advantage.

Prayer for the Day

I pray for guidance and liberation to rightly use my resources to my advantage. I will no longer squander my time or energies with passive, wishful thinking. I pray to fully acknowledge and to rightly use my strengths without guilt or regret.

Mantra for the Day

    I free myself to use my resources. I free myself to use my resources. I free myself to use my resources.

Reflection for the day

_____

_____

_____

_____

_____

_____

_____

_____

_____

_____

_____

_____

_____

_____

_____

_____

_____

Thought for the day

Woman is the true giver of life. We give life, we nurture life, and we bring joy to life. I will not be the slave to the slaves. I will not subject myself to the appraisal of men. How often have women been demoralized for being intelligent? How often have women been derided for a physical appearance that does not match the perverse, lascivious perspective of immature males? I no longer tolerate this ungracious treatment of myself or my sisters. I rise above this behavior that is intended to keep the 'woman in her place', and I claim my rightful place as queen. I no longer lend my precious time or energies to the stupidity that once defined the battle of the sexes. There is no battle or room for discussion; women have and always will be superior! Who is there to comfort a man when he has fears or is in pain? Certainly not another man! They come to us when they feel weak because they know we are strong and provide comfort and direction.

Meditation for the day

I contemplate my true worth without the evaluation of the former patriarchal standards that attempted to stifle me. I define my worth. I prove my intellect and take pride in my abilities. I am as God made me. This brings me peace as I'm sure the Supreme is pleased with me. Who wouldn't be happy with an independent woman of strength and compassion?

Prayer for the day

I pray to be given the strength to rise above the contemptuous behaviors that have been directed toward me in the past. I pray Divine guidance that I can turn the past to good account. I seek to lift men by promoting their success rather than devaluing them. As a woman raises her awareness of her personal worth, all around her will benefit.

Mantra for the day

It is a new world, and I am free from the past. It is a new world, and I am free from the past. It is a new world, and I am free from the past.

Reflection for the day

_____

_____

_____

_____

_____

_____

_____

_____

_____

_____

_____

_____

_____

Thought for the Day
Our power does indeed come both
spiritually and from within. One can not take power
from anyone else. Even the people that come into
our lives to make them easier are not giving up their
power. In fact we are empowering them. I have
come to believe that equality does not provide the
life balance that I seek. Just as some women have
latent desires to lead, other people have suppressed
their desires to follow. We can see that when these
two people come together they will have much in
common. When this match can be made and all of
the little subtleties of power exchange worked out,
great things will come to pass. Too many people
get caught up in the improper exchange of power
and the use of negative manipulation. When all
parties agree on who is in charge of the relationship,
all of the negative energy that was going into
personal power struggles can be harnesses and put
to a positive use that will rapidly benefit all
concerned. As a female it is in my best interest to
fully facilitate our roles so that everyone can live to
their full potential.

Meditation for the Day
I look back at the fallacy of equality. How
much energy did I expend trying to balance his
feelings with my needs? I also see the depth of my
emotional wounds as I tried to compromise my
well-being in an effort to maintain peace. As I ever
evolve as an enlightened woman of power, I now
fully realize that my days of self-sacrifice and
suffering are over. I am desirable and they will
seek me out for my beauty, strength and the
freedom that I can provide.

Prayer for the Day

I ask that I be given the insight I need to promote well-being among the people in my life. Recognizing my strengths, I will seek to rightly use them to further bring peace into our lives.

Mantra for the Day

Equality is not balance. Equality is not balance. Equality is not balance.

Reflection for the day

_____

_____

_____

_____

_____

_____

_____

_____

_____

_____

_____

_____

_____

Thought for the day

Men's rights are nothing more. Women's rights are nothing less. -- Susan B. Anthony

What a wonderful, simplistic way to look at life! Yes indeed, the boys are ahead at this juncture. We, as women, cannot hold ourselves responsible for the past but we need to take on personal accountability for the future. Each one of us can begin to stand up against injustice. No longer is it necessary to quietly endure social injustice and lack of accountability. Speak up, tell your sisters, write a letter to the editor, get involved locally and vote. The changes we want to see personally and socially will only come to fruition through hard work and sacrifice. I am the one responsible for my life. If I want it changed I must do the work to promote change. I am ready to work.

Meditation for the day

I look back through history and see what measures were used to restrain women's growth. Lack of education always limits potential. Finances and lack of childcare limited our ability to move freely in society. As a group of enlightened women, let us ban together to meet each other's needs so that we all can grow. Take time to watch someone else's children so she can go to school. Make a commitment to love and support another woman you know so that she, too, can grow to reach her potential.

Prayer for the day

I pray to find my voice of resistance and couple it with my heart full of hope. I am sure my Creator has endowed me with the power to influence personal and societal changes. I ask to wisely use this power to encourage growth in another woman.

Mantra for the day

I am busy working for change. I am busy working for change. I am busy working for change.

Reflection for the day

_____

_____

_____

_____

_____

_____

_____

_____

_____

_____

_____

_____

Thought for the day

If men were truly the superior sex there would be no need to suppress women. Why is there a patriarchal effort to control a woman's dress, her employment, and her freedom to excel? All control comes from fear. Is it possible that men realize their own inferiority and powerlessness before an enlightened woman? Do they seek to control her to avoid the truth? Men fear women for they realize her superiority in matters of intellect and emotion. Men attempt to control because they fully realize the power of woman and her irresistible attraction. Men attempt to control and limit women because they cannot control and limit their own actions or desires. Women are superior and today we all know it.

Meditation for the day

Today I contemplate the truth of my superiority. By birth and hard work, I have created a powerful force that will be recognized and supported. When I can fully recognize and acknowledge my worth, others will see it as well. It is not strange that others seek to encourage and support me, for I am worthy.

Prayer for the day

I ask to ever be worthy of my position in life. I will always strive to promote and not restrict others. I am superior to man and I will show that superiority through love and compassion. I seek to encourage and not to restrict for we all need to grow to our full potential.

Mantra for the day

Superior women work for the betterment of all. Superior women work for the betterment of all. Superior women work for the betterment of all.

Reflection for the day

_____

_____

_____

_____

_____

_____

_____

_____

_____

_____

_____

_____

_____

_____

_____

_____

_____

Thought for the day

The only limits I have on my power and growth are those I place upon myself. Having been in a number of abusive relationships in the past, I continually saw myself as a victim. I often wondered if I had an invisible sign on my forehead that read, 'abuse me; help yourself.' Actually I did; it was my demeanor; how I presented myself to the world. Lacking confidence and self-assuredness, that sign was visible to every predator within a fifty-mile radius. I easily fell into that role when the confident and arrogant man came along to rescue me from my 'miserable existence.' And I was ever so grateful! In my growth as a person and a woman, I have removed that sign. By setting my own goals and working to achieve those, I have been able to build a life of my choosing. With each goal accomplished, no matter how small, my belief in myself grows. Today I understand and accept that my life has limits, but most of the limits are ones I have set, not someone else.

Meditation for the day

I choose to see myself differently today. I am a strong and capable woman with awesome gifts to offer. Today, it is not so important to be rescued as it is to build and grow a strong sense of self through my effort. Today I focus on the progress made and the direction I choose to continue growing.

Prayer for the day

I offer thanks for the support and wisdom in choosing the limits I place and the direction in which I grow. I pray for continued guidance and strength to build the woman that may offer the same to others.

Mantra for the day

Today I can rescue myself. Today I can rescue myself. Today I can rescue myself.

Reflection for the day

_____

_____

_____

_____

_____

_____

_____

_____

_____

_____

_____

_____

_____

_____

_____

Thought for the day

I once made a statement to a friend that I was open-minded. Her response was simply 'no you are not'. The discussion continued with her knowing smile, and in kind voice she once again responded by saying that 'I was not open-minded, but rather I was broad-minded'. My defense; 'it's the same thing; open-minded and broad-minded'. I told her I was a staunch supporter of freedom and personal rights. I went on to say that everyone had the right to think and do as they will. My rant continued with an oration on freedom that fell just short of anarchy. Her kindly response, 'no, you are...broad-minded'. In frustration I queried;' what then would the difference be'? With kindness and love she smiled and said, 'if you were really open-minded you'd be willing to change.' Ouch!

Meditation for the day

Today I meditate on the difference between dispassionate broad-mindedness, and passion-filled open-mindedness. I choose to pursue passion, stand on willingness, and reach for the changes that give me hope and faith.

Prayer for the day

I pray for willingness and discernment so I can open my heart and mind to true change. I want true change, not apathetic self-righteousness and smugness. A broad mind is a mind closed to personal fulfillment and usefulness.

Mantra for the day

I am open-minded and willing to change. I am open-minded and willing to change. I am open-minded and willing to change.

Reflection for the day

_____

_____

_____

_____

_____

_____

_____

_____

_____

_____

_____

_____

_____

_____

_____

_____

_____

Thought for the day

I am God's girl. I do not now and never will belong to a man again. My gifts, my pleasure, and my purpose come from above. I must always remember the Source of my strength. As God's girl I relish the strength that is bestowed upon me, I cherish these gifts and will not let anyone interfere in Our relationship. I seek, I serve, I receive, and I am made whole.

Meditation for the day

Today I look back and view the folly that my life once was. I see that my reliance was on men, not on God. My needs were not met, my growth was minimal, and my soul seized with sadness. Today I refuse to let anyone <u>EVER</u> take from me again. They have taken enough. I thought that I was giving, but no; I was being robbed. I've worked hard to achieve my station in life and I rebuff any efforts to demean my person. Today I focus on myself as a queen, and as a goddess. I control what emotions I absorb and dispense. I am not subordinate to whim or pettiness. I rule my realm and only acknowledge those who respect me.

Prayer for the day

Today I pray to always be cognizant of the gift of God's love. I pray that I will never lower myself to the point that I once considered a meaningful existence. I pray that I continue to glory in my power and use it to guide others to a better more meaningful life.

Mantra for the day

I am God's girl; my service is to my
Spiritual Guide. I am God's girl; my service is to
my Spiritual Guide.

Reflection for the day

_____

_____

_____

_____

_____

_____

_____

_____

_____

_____

_____

_____

_____

_____

_____

_____

Thought for the day

It seems that whenever I find myself 'lost' in life I scramble all the harder to find meaning. This would appear to be wasted time and energy. Today I realize that my efforts to find meaning in any situation are simply a veiled attempt to control it. In essence, if I know what is going on then I'll know what to do. I burn up a lot of energy trying to understand situations that are often founded on untruths and falsehoods. If there is one thing that I am certain of it is this; I need to learn how to live free in this life. One of the greatest freedoms that I'll ever have is my freedom not to wrestle fearful situations to the ground to control them. Life is just life; it is here and we are here to enjoy it, not to control it. Both my need to find meaning and my need to control come from my fears.

Meditation for the day

Today I contemplate on how fear has driven me to find meaning and to seek control. The more I lose control, the more I seek to control. In other words, the more I fear, the more I fear. I need to know and believe at depth that my faith, in God and in myself, is the only thing that can break this vicious cycle of self-defeat.

Prayer for the day

I pray that my faith will override my fears and need for control. As an enlightened woman I am here to interact, help and lead others, not to fall victim to fear. I pray to live in this day with a freedom that enables me to be non-controlling and useful to all.

Mantra for the day

Faith overcomes fear. Faith overcomes fear.
Faith overcomes fear.

Reflection for the day

_____

_____

_____

_____

_____

_____

_____

_____

_____

_____

_____

_____

_____

_____

_____

_____

_____

_____

Thought for the day

As women we are expected to be emotionally strong at all times. We are the emotional and spiritual leaders in our homes and our relationships. We carry and comfort children without complaint. We heal broken men when the pains and struggles of life have reduced them to tears. Women also comfort and hold each other for they know it is better to cry with another woman than to cry alone. The land of tears can be a very lonely place if we don't seek out a friend to share with. The great strength of a woman is that she can emotionally bend without breaking. She knows that tomorrow will be another day and she looks forward to once more utilizing her faith, her strength, and her heart to heal herself and those that she loves. A woman is a very powerful, helpful force even when she bends under the weight of love for she knows that she has the love of her God to strengthen and guide her.

Meditation for the day

As a queen I know that I will never surrender or break under the stresses of life and love. In the past and I'm sure that in the future as well I will once again taste my own tears. I need not doubt myself for I know two very important facts. The first is that everything needs water to grow. The second is that those tears are NOT weakness; they are only pain leaving my body.

Prayer for the day

I pray to find comfort in my tears. I pray to recognize the fact that one woman cannot be expected to carry the pain of many. My tears can

and often will create a new and wonderful bond
with another understanding woman.

Mantra for the day
  Tears do not diminish my power. Tears do
not diminish my power. Tears do not diminish my
power.

Reflection for the day

Thought for the day

It is said that our strength comes from our trials in life. When we think about women's rights, various images may come to mind. We may think about voting rights, burning bras, women's firsts: the first woman doctor, lawyer, writer, senator, astronaut, presidential candidate. Our daughters may take these roles for granted because they grew up seeing them played out in everyday life. It is important to remember the struggle, however. The trials of life do keep us strong and our continued valor is needed for further evolution of women as a people of heroism. And there is so much farther to go.

Meditation for the day

I gain my strength for today from the trials of my sisters in the past. My focus today is growth. I am strong and have wisdom of the past to guide my future. I will listen and use that wisdom accordingly.

Prayer for the day

Our most Supreme Strengthener, please give us resolution as a collective whole to continue to move forward in our journey. Help us to use the wisdom and fortitude provided to make our existence one that will breed even stronger women in the days to come. Thank you for that strength and wisdom.

Mantra for the day

We have a voice that we must use wisely. We have a voice that we must use wisely. We have a voice that we must use wisely.

Reflection for the day

_____

_____

_____

_____

_____

_____

_____

_____

_____

_____

_____

_____

_____

_____

_____

_____

_____

Thought for the day

This is the day that God has given me. I choose to honor the Creator by honoring myself. I will care for my body, clear my mind of negativity, open my heart to the goodness of the universe, and share my talents as I believe God would have me. I'll no longer be an apathetic play-thing for unthinking, uncaring males. By honoring myself, my Creator will be pleased. This, in turn, fulfills me. My satisfaction comes from my relationship with my God, not from a man. However, man can *only* be fulfilled through the power of a woman. Man is most a man when a woman shares herself with him. A man defines himself by the woman he is with. A man will not reach his full capacity without the warmth and strength of an enlightened woman. It is her goodness, her grace, her power that will enable him to rise to his full potential.

Meditation for the day

Today I recognize my power and embrace it. The very feelings that used to bring me fear now bring me comfort. I no longer need to fear my intellectual or emotional power or the lust that my power promotes in males. Men are drawn to strength; I have the strength that they seek and admire. I use my power to promote myself and my sisters. Together the power of women will enable the more enlightened males to find fulfillment in their service of womankind; service that males long to render but are often too weak to admit. The strength of a woman is needed to guide, promote, and bring to the surface the true nature of man. This truth will free him of centuries of deceit and happily place him at the foot of women where he longs to be.

Prayer for the day

I pray that I may make peace with the power that God has given me. I pray that I no longer fear my power. I ask that I learn to use my power in concert with the power of the universe. I pray that I may use it wisely to promote the lives of everyone I meet.

Mantra for the day

I do not fear my power it is God's gift to me. I do not fear my power it is God's gift to me. I do not fear my power it is God's gift to me.

Reflection for the day

_____

_____

_____

_____

_____

_____

_____

_____

_____

_____

_____

_____

Thought for the day

I've never been overly fond of male aggression and callousness. I have been on the receiving end of this behavior and found it to be tremendously distasteful. It's important to remember that as I grow, I need to chart a path for my ascent. I want to grow in the spirit of my Creator. I want to be recognized for true power; the God-given power of love. I want to aspire to softness of word and deed. I should never have cause to raise my voice. There is great strength in loving kindness and gentle expression. My power lies in the peace that flows through me. I share this God given peace with those in my life. I want to guide with the compassion of a woman, not the callousness of a man. I desire to be a leader of peace.

Meditation for the day

I do not want to lead with fear and force. The aggression of the patriarchal society of the past has led only to fear, failure and discord. People that are selfishly dominated are never free to grow. However, everyone is free to follow a pioneer that promotes harmony and well-being. It is not so much who you guide as how you guide that will determine your course through life.

Prayer for the day

I pray to not foolishly follow in the failed leadership of the past. I pray to realize that a woman's true worth is never found in the failed patriarchal passions of the past. I pray to be attractive in my efforts to share the gifts that have been freely given to me.

Mantra for the day

My compassion guides me. My compassion guides me. My compassion guides me.

Reflection for the day

_____

_____

_____

_____

_____

_____

_____

_____

_____

_____

_____

_____

_____

_____

_____

_____

Thought for the day

Receiving help and kindness is one of the hardest lessons to learn. I find it quite easy to give help to others but very difficult to receive the blessings my friends offer. When I accept help from someone else I erroneously classify my feelings as feelings of defeat. The truth is that when I offer help to another I never view them as deficient, I'm just grateful for the opportunity to be helpful. In order to graciously receive, I first need to give up my control of the situation. I also need to resign as score keeper and give my benefactor the same freedom to be useful and to grow. If I can view my reception of aid as an opportunity for growth for both of us, I'll be much better off. If I truly wish to grow and be useful, I will learn about the other side of giving. I will seek to be a gracious recipient as well as a grateful contributor. I will seize the opportunity to grow in humility.

Meditation for the day

My growth needs to be well rounded. I cannot always be the one that gives to another. Sometimes it is in everyone's best interest if I just sit back and let someone else glory in success. Learning to receive is not an exercise in humiliation; it is an opportunity to grow in humility. It is important to keep myself centered and not become haughty. I will allow everyone opportunities for growth and success.

Prayer for the day

I pray to walk a humble path with my friends and before my God. The path of humility is the path of strength and character. I pray to graciously be a humble recipient of love, kindness, and direction.

Mantra for the day
> My humble path leads to spiritual growth. My humble path leads to spiritual growth. My humble path leads to spiritual growth.

Reflection for the day

_____

_____

_____

_____

_____

_____

_____

_____

_____

_____

_____

_____

_____

_____

_____

Thought for the day

It seems that I have always had a strained relationship with pain and sorrow. One of the greatest difficulties in dealing with these emotions is that I have either felt unworthy of joy or have resisted the lesson that comes with pain. Often given the choice of working through and accepting these feelings, I have chosen not to do the work and allowed fear to push me into a state of apathy. When I am apathetic, I simply don't care or have an opinion. I am therefore lacking in passion. Passion is what needs to drive me. I cannot afford to live without passion, for it overrides fear that can keep me paralyzed. If and when I choose to park my emotions with apathy, all of the forward progress in my life stops.

Meditation for the day

Today, I recognize that apathy is the worst of human emotions. I look to the past and see the terrible destructiveness that apathy affords. Passion is the result of my spiritual connection. All passion comes from love; all love comes from God. I need to keep my life alive with the love and passion that my God offers.

Prayer for the day

I pray to maintain the passion of a queen. I pray that my spiritual condition will draw people to me so that I will be allowed to share my love and strength with them. I pray to seek and passionately do the will of my God. A goddess serves so that she may be passionately served and the circle of life and love fulfilled.

Mantra for the day
  I live with passion. I live with passion. I
live with passion.

Reflection for the day

_____

_____

_____

_____

_____

_____

_____

_____

_____

_____

_____

_____

_____

_____

_____

Thought for the day

During the dating process the woman is seen by the man as being worthy of pursuit. He wines and dines her; bends over backward to meet her desires in an effort to win her affections. She is seen as being worth working for, and he enhances his self-esteem by pleasing her. Once the relationship is formed and the woman is viewed as an equal, the gifts and dinners often stop and romance is replaced by sex. Most men will not evolve beyond this point without the guidance of a knowledgeable woman. The strong enlightened woman of today will not accept an assignment of apathetic equality; she will strive to maintain her position of eminence for the betterment of all.

Meditation for the day

I consciously resist all patriarchal efforts to reduce myself to equality. I was born a princess and through dedicated effort have risen to the position of queen. I will not reduce my stature for love. The kindest, most loving act is to raise his position not to lower mine. We are never be equal but with my loving guidance, we can avoid the mundane attitudes that destroy so many relationships. When he strives to please me, he is made whole. I learn to graciously receive the love and attention of another. I will remain special and worthy of his time, effort and pursuit.

Prayer for the day

I ask to be ever mindful of my position of eminence in this journey through life. When I aspire to be the proud and beautiful daughter of my Creator, I can be most useful to all. I set a positive example for my sisters of what a spiritually fulfilled woman can do.

Mantra for the day

    I will not surrender my position for love. I will not surrender my position for love. I will not surrender my position for love.

Reflection for the day

_____

_____

_____

_____

_____

_____

_____

_____

_____

_____

_____

_____

_____

_____

_____

_____

_____

Thought for the day

He asks me out; I say yes or no. He wants to kiss; I say yes or no. He wants to touch; I say yes or no. He wants to do other things; I say yes or no. He wants to get married; I say yes or no. Looks like I've *always* had the power and the control. It makes me wonder why I never realized this before. Even society acknowledges the power of a woman's choice in these matters. If a man dares to do anything without a woman's consent, society takes a stand against his actions. I have all of the power and I have all of the control until I give it away. I will no longer give it away.

Meditation for the day

I ponder why a woman is compelled to give up her personal control. It seems that as soon as she is in a relationship, she trades all of her power and most of her rights simply to be with a man. This is a man that had to fight and struggle to be noticed by her in the first place. As women we need to rewrite this romance novel and make sure that the balance of power remains at our command. This is how we can be assured of a happy ending in our own story. The male needs to evermore seek the attention of the female; his thirst for conquest should never be fully satisfied. He needs to continuously work for us and our benefit.

Prayer for the day

I pray to be fully aware of my true position in the battle of the sexes. I ask that I can continuously remember that he seeks me, and he seeks my approval of him. I pray to never feel diminished before the eyes of a man again. When I can see the truth for what it is, there is no doubt that I have the power, for I control the treasure he seeks.

Mantra for the day

I am the treasure, not him. I am the treasure, not him. I am the treasure, not him.

Reflection for the day

_____

_____

_____

_____

_____

_____

_____

_____

_____

_____

_____

_____

_____

_____

_____

Thought for the day

Whenever a male starts a new job he can expect to receive training, possibly attend seminars and receive guidance from his superiors. When a man plays sports there is always a coach to help him improve his natural abilities. In this regard males are used to and expect direction. When, however, the decision is made to enter into a relationship with a woman, he is arrogant enough to think that he needs no instruction. Being with the woman he loves SHOULD be the most important decision that he will ever make. Wouldn't you think he should be expected to receive some training here as well? If the woman does not recognize her true worth and insist on guiding him, he cannot be successful. When we look at the above examples we can see that a male is conditioned to receive guidance. After all, his training did begin with his mother! When a couple becomes a couple there is no singular focus; the focus must be on the greater good for all. With the proper tutelage from an enlightened woman a man can be transformed from a selfish, ego driven male into worthwhile mate.

Meditation for the day

I can see the role and importance that training has for a man. He has been conditioned to work hard to achieve his goals and be successful. As an enlightened woman, I must not deny his conditioning so that he may attain his goals for success with me. Without my help a man will continue to be self destructive and hurtful. I will be the coach and teach him how to develop into the man that he has always wanted to be.

Prayer for the day

I pray to see the female and male roles in a new light. I desire to let the light of the truth invade the darkness of patriarchy and lies. I pray for strength and guidance in my leadership role.

Mantra for the day

I was born to lead. I was born to lead. I was born to lead.

Reflection for the day

_____

_____

_____

_____

_____

_____

_____

_____

_____

_____

_____

_____

_____

_____

_____

Thought for the day

We must not fear our shadow for the Light is always at hand. There are times that I have doubted myself, my goodness and my values. This usually happens when I am self-absorbed and not conscious of the Light that is always nearby. My God provides the light that I need to be the shadow. Whatever I believe to be my Creator's wants and desires, that is how I should act. I need to make every effort to be a mirror of God's wishes. Just as my own shadow follows me, my shadow will also follow my Creator. It is important to act in concert with the Spirit's desires and actions. My love is a reflection of this; forgiving as I am also forgiven. By being a shadow to my God's wishes my life will continue to improve for the Light will always be seen.

Meditation for the day

I no longer seek or live in the darkness of my own spirit. I seek to live in the Light of my Creator's spirit. Lies and deceit cannot live in the Light. For my personal good and for the good of all and everyone I love, I strive to move toward the Light and the glory.

Prayer for the day

I pray to be a shadow of my God. I ask that my thoughts, words, and deeds are a reflection of all of the goodness that is shared with me. There cannot be a shadow without Light. I pray to bask in the Light to let my shadow glow with love.

Mantra for the day

Only with Light can my shadow be seen.
Only with Light can my shadow be seen. Only with
Light can my shadow be seen.

Reflection for the day

_____

_____

_____

_____

_____

_____

_____

_____

_____

_____

_____

_____

_____

_____

_____

_____

Thought for the day

Sometimes our busy lives and our desire to help others can keep us from taking care of ourselves properly. We need to be aware or our personal needs and take the time to find self-fulfillment. For some it will be travel or quiet time with a book; for others it might be doing a little writing or catching up on correspondence. Crafting can be an excellent way to find and provide self-expression and personal satisfaction. It would seem that everyone likes to see and share items that are created with a personal touch. Personal time and heartfelt creations are wonderful ways to create and share the love that we feel for ourselves and others.

Meditation for the day

I make sure to take time for myself. Sometimes I need to rearrange my schedule or raise my expectations of others so that through their efforts I have the time that I deserve. I look within to discover my personal needs. Then I can take the action necessary to provide the time and materials necessary to produce a well-deserved break from the rigors of daily life. I make time and properly care for myself because I am worth it.

Prayer for the day

I ask for the willingness and the opportunities to take care of myself. I ask to be free from guilt so that I may find a little time to recharge my soul through learning and self-expression. Please help me to feel comforted in my decision to put myself first for a change.

Mantra for the day

I am worth taking care of. I am worth
taking care of. I am worth taking care of.

Reflection for the day

_____

_____

_____

_____

_____

_____

_____

_____

_____

_____

_____

_____

_____

_____

_____

_____

Thought for the day

Love, love, love. We all want to be in love. Experience and age has shown me that to be in 'like' is far more beneficial that being in love. The truth demands that I share this next statement. I have been in love with people I couldn't stand! What a dreadful position in which to find yourself. If we can establish our 'like' before we fall in 'love' we'll have a much more productive and peaceful relationship. Wouldn't it make more sense to find our 'love' based on shared values, common causes, and shared beliefs? What good would it do to find a 'love' that didn't share my thoughts on women's true place in society as a leader? He needs to like the fact that *I AM* the queen.

Meditation for the day

The passion of love is a two way street. The best measure of passion is the level of intensity that we feel in our lives. In this regard, passion can be every bit as bad as it is good. Likewise, 'love' can be every bit as bad as it is good. 'Like' on the other hand provides the foundation for a lasting relationship with the promise for more good and less bad. I want to like my love, and I want him to like me enough to love.

Prayer for the day

I pray to reorganize my thinking to be free from the hold of fairy tale love and passion. I expand my communication skills so I can learn to like my partner. I pray for a rational mind to see if we are compatible in order that my 'like' can override my former flawed views of love and passion.

Mantra for the day
    I love 'like'. I love 'like'. I love 'like'.

Reflection for the day

_____

_____

_____

_____

_____

_____

_____

_____

_____

_____

_____

_____

_____

_____

_____

_____

_____

Thought for the day

It has been said that acceptance is receiving without resistance. If this is true, it becomes apparent that I have had a problem with acceptance for years. It must be part of the 'good girl' training that I received in my youth. However, I still have difficulties accepting compliments and the goodness that is due me. When acknowledged for my abilities how often do I demure? Or say things like; 'oh it was nothing anyone could have done it'. I need to learn to accept the goodness and accolades that this world and people have been trying to share with me. I need to receive without resistance. When I can say without reservation that I am worthy, I am a queen and a goddess; my acceptance will be at a much higher level.

Meditation for the day

Today I contemplate my resistance to accept what has always been mine to claim. Today I receive all the love and goodness that a woman of my stature deserves. I accept my power, my light, and my new way of life as any queen would accept the gifts brought before her. In the past I was taught how to give, which can be quite fulfilling. Now, I need to teach myself how to receive and accept so that the natural balance is found. When I rightly see myself I am able to receive from others and provide for their fulfillment.

Prayer for the day

I pray that the Creative Force remove my resistance to receive. Today I believe that this Force wants me to have all of the goodness available to me. I pray to disengage myself from the false pride that has limited me. I replace it with true pride so I may rightly acknowledge my gifts.

Mantra for the day
        I receive without resistance. I receive without resistance. I receive without resistance.

Reflection for the day

_____

_____

_____

_____

_____

_____

_____

_____

_____

_____

_____

_____

_____

_____

_____

_____

Thought for the day

Courage! I've often heard this word rightly used to describe our war heroes and public servants. Make no mistake those brave men and women are ALL heroes. However, I seldom think of my own personal courage and how best to apply it's use to my life. It is said that courage is fear that has said its prayers. Unfortunately, courage and fear do co-exist. Valor is mine to claim only when I take actions in spite of the pain and fear that this world has caused me. The willingness to take action, the willingness to promote positive change in the face of paralyzing fear is courage. The courage I seek already resides within me. My strength comes from my indomitable nature, and my spiritual connection. My innate strength and the power of God provide all the courage I'll ever need. I've said my prayers I have courage. I have no reason to fear myself, people or change.

Meditation for the day

I reflect and see that I have moved through pain and fear before. I need to see these two antagonists not as inhibiters but as promoters of my courage. I have faith and I need always to remember that all people of faith are people of courage. I fear not. I am my own hero!

Prayer for the day

I pray to always be conscious of my faith and courage. I pray to never separate myself from the position of spiritual advantage that I now enjoy. I pray to use the goodness of my spirit and the will of my God to promote courage in those less fortunate than me. I ask God to grant me the strength to provide a safe haven for others.

Mantra for the day

I have and will continue to have all the courage that I need. I have and continue to have all the courage that I need. I have and will continue to have all the courage that I need.

Reflection for the day

_____

_____

_____

_____

_____

_____

_____

_____

_____

_____

_____

_____

_____

_____

_____

_____

Thought for the day

Perceptions are not reality. In our society, men are often conditioned to put forth a particular image. This image allows them to fit in with 'masculine' expectations that were formed many, many years ago. With the advent of 'equality' of the sexes, however, many are left with a confusion regarding their roles. It is useful therefore to provide outlines so that all may be successful in their perspective roles. In a 'traditional' family the male works and woman remains at home to rule the roost. In a female led relationship, the woman not only rules the roost but every other aspect of their lives. When a man is free from the dictates of the patriarchal society, he is open to express his love and devotion in appropriate ways. With this type of freedom, he is allowed to be more creative, attentive and loving. Socially he may be the one out there barking, but it is she who is holding the leash!

Meditation for the day

Today I realize the strength of women will change the world. Through her men are offered a direction and freedom not previously available. When we all stand united under one purpose, one God, we will grow into a power that will allow us to withstand the storms of life. When the driving force of life is love and not arrogance, our spirits will be united for our common purpose; love, peace and fulfillment.

Prayer for the day

I pray today to have the strength and wisdom to offer direction in a loving and considerate way. I ask to show courage and determination to allow freedom for others in my life. I offer thanks for the many blessings provided.

Mantra for the day
  I have a new 'leash' on life. I have a new 'leash' on life. I have a new 'leash' on life. ☺

Reflection for the day

_____

_____

_____

_____

_____

_____

_____

_____

_____

_____

_____

_____

_____

_____

_____

_____

Thought for the day

Affirmation. If I am going to move into a new and more meaningful life, first and foremost I must believe that I am capable, and deserving of achieving my goals. I affirm myself though the thoughtful care that I provide myself. I treat my body, mind, and soul as the treasures that they are. I take the time that I need to educate myself and set achievable goals. I reexamine my path on a regular basis and repeatedly acknowledge my capacity to excel. Throughout the day I tell myself that I am doing well. I've replaced the old defeatist negativity with positive self-talk. I compliment myself on my appearance and my abilities. I affirm my belief system and express pleasure in my pure motives and the kindness of my heart. I actively treat myself as I would gladly treat anyone else. I tell myself that I am deserving of all the goodness that this life has to offer. I act on my positive thoughts.

Meditation for the day

I concentrate on how I positively address myself today. My self-talk will be void of negativity and conflict. I am the architect of my thoughts and actions. I never fail in my efforts to treat myself with dignity, compassion, and respect. I am on a fabulous journey to self-realization; I will not accept false direction.

Prayer for the day

I pray to constantly be kind with myself. I pray to remember that I too need positive affirmation and warmth. I pray to realize my true self as I walk with God on my journey of life. I pray for the ability to love myself as my God loves me. Today we apply the love that I need to feel fulfilled and unceasingly pursue my dreams

Mantra for the day
  I am kind, capable, beautiful and deserving. I am kind, capable, beautiful and deserving. I am kind, capable, beautiful, and deserving.

Reflection for the day

_____

_____

_____

_____

_____

_____

_____

_____

_____

_____

_____

_____

_____

_____

_____

Thought for the day

This newness, this change into becoming an empowered woman seems a little odd at first. One set of voices says; 'no way, you just can't create a new life', but the reality is that we can and do fabricate our existence each and every everyday. With the choices we make we are constantly creating our world. We all have the freedom to choose better. The problem up to this point is we have been evolving in a very small world under the ever watchful eye of an archaic patriarchal society. Life is all about deciding who we are then living in that creation. The one person who is most responsible for my limited growth is me! I need to dream, I need to believe, I need to become. I am a goddess trapped in a sparse existence waiting for my own permission to embrace the life of my choosing. I do grant permission!

Meditation for the day

Today I consider my resistance to my own personal growth. Do I have fears of upsetting the patriarchs? Do I not believe deeply enough in myself and the sisterhood? Do I doubt my strength and the perseverance it will take to facilitate my ascent? Do I lack the fundamental belief that God wants me to rise to my full potential? What holds me back?

Prayer for the day

Today I pray for my own liberation from the constraints of my limited lifestyle choices. I pray for the power to embrace the future with a change in outlook and action. I pray to become what I never really believed I could, but always knew I was; a strong and independent woman of substance.

Mantra for the day

   My growth is limitless. My growth is
limitless. My growth is limitless.

Reflection for the day

_____

_____

_____

_____

_____

_____

_____

_____

_____

_____

_____

_____

_____

_____

_____

_____

_____

Thought for the day

I don't need new things, I need a new vision. So many times I have changed my circumstances instead of refocusing my vision. The old Biblical adage of turn the other cheek comes to mind. With the way I'm thinking today this statement takes on a whole new meaning. If you would; quiet your mind and visualize turning the other cheek. What happens? Your head swivels and a whole new world will come into view! When the pain, sorrow, sadness or disappointments of life face me, I no longer need to run. Today I can simply explore my options and either find or create a new vision. As an enlightened woman, the world is mine to create. I do not run from uncomfortable circumstances. I visualize peace and quietly reconstruct my reality. I will create a new vision for my life, not look for a new existence. I'm tired of starting over; I want to redefine the life I have.

Meditation for the day

Running away and starting over are no longer viable options for me. Each time I give up it feels like someone else wins. A woman does not surrender to the difficulties of life; she surmounts all obstacles with grace and dignity. I overcome the arduous trials of my life with new energy and vision. I create the world that I want as my own. I do not allow interference or transgressions. I do not yield to my old behavior patterns. New vision will create new victory.

Prayer for the day

I pray to be empowered to visualize all my possibilities. I ask for patience as a creator of this vision. I pray for strength and fortitude to meet the demands I place on myself. I pray to have an active hand in my destiny.

Mantra for the day
     I have faith in my capabilities as a visionary. I have faith in my capabilities as a visionary. I have faith in my capabilities as a visionary.

Reflection for the day

_____

_____

_____

_____

_____

_____

_____

_____

_____

_____

_____

_____

_____

_____

_____

_____

Thought for the day

We've all heard it before; once the words leave your mouth there is no taking them back. Not only have we heard this, we have also felt the sting and hurt words can have when delivered, whether innocently or maliciously. Conversely, we have all hurt others through our neglectful use of thought, word and deed. Here is where we can practice the change that we wish to promote. If we soften our heart and purge ourselves of hurtful attitudes, we'll be far less likely to commit these offenses. When I can expand my sphere of consciousness to be inclusive rather than exclusive I'm on my way to successful change. In the past, I have looked for differences and separation leading to the possibility of judging others. When I do this, my negative judgments are often followed by negative and hurtful commentary. This is not the way of a truly enlightened woman.

Meditation for the day

Today I look to be inclusive. I seek opportunities to free my mind by liberating it from the caustic judgments that have plagued me in the past. When I look for commonality I can be inclusive. I am far less likely to judge others when we share similar beliefs and feelings. It is important for me to meet my sisters and brothers on the field of love and understanding, not the battlefield of anger and indifference.

Prayer for the day

Today I pray to be granted the vision that I seek allowing me to find commonality. I pray in times of turmoil my heart will rise to the occasion and override the erroneous thoughts and judgments

I may have. I ask that my words will be tempered with the kindness and loving concern that my heart seeks to share with everyone.

Mantra for the day
      I can love people whether I like them or not. I can love people whether I like them or not. I can love people whether I like them or not.

Reflection for the day

_____

_____

_____

_____

_____

_____

_____

_____

_____

_____

_____

_____

_____

_____

Thought for the day

What is a goddess anyway? The power and control of a queen is appealing to many. The idea of allowing a submissive man to serve is very affirming. How do I go about promoting the changes that I seek? It will take a combination of all the things we've been talking about. A new life requires new thought, new belief, positive action, and of course, a new attitude. A self-assured woman will draw submissive men to her. As she walks, men will see her assertiveness. As she talks, they will hear her self-worth and feel the kindness of her love. A queen does not need to raise her voice or experience anxiety. She is self-assured in her position. We've all seen powerful people before, they almost radiate vibrations that attract people to them. It is a state of mind; it is an attitude, a spiritual connection that is easily recognized. Once our personal power is established, it can provide for us and our needs.

Meditation for the day

I need to always remember that as a goddess I am not better than anyone else. I also need to recognize that as a goddess I am much better than I was! I've always had the power; I was unable to recognize that it was mine to claim. Today I claim my power. I have the power to set myself free and to guide those that seek me out.

Prayer for the day

I pray to recognize my true potential as a woman of power. I ask to know in my heart and not doubt my unlimited potential for compassion and leadership. I pray to carry myself and treat myself as the woman my God intended me to be. I pray for my growth so I can recognize and develop fully as a queen.

Mantra for the day

    I no longer doubt my potential. I no longer doubt my potential. I no longer doubt my potential.

Reflection for the day

_____

_____

_____

_____

_____

_____

_____

_____

_____

_____

_____

_____

_____

_____

_____

_____

_____

Thought for the day

How very easy it is to get caught up in the greed of this world and believe that I can define me or my success by earthly possessions. It needs to be clear to all that our primary goal for this life is to be useful. The best way to honor the Creator is to honor the Divine children. There are many people that we can help. Often, all it takes is a minute of our time or a kind word. Smiles are still free and one of the most beautiful pleasures this life has to offer. One of our primary purposes should be to seek to be free from the dictates of our self-will. Many people fail to realize that we cannot overcome self alone; we need to have people to help us. When I reach out to another with a pure motive I am actively working to free myself from the selfishness that seeks to own me. I cannot serve myself and my God at the same time. I must choose who will be my Master.

Meditation for the day

I will try to see the positive aspects of being free from self. It seems odd that freeing ones self from the bondage of self should be my primary goal in life but all spiritual progress requires a degree of humility. I am not useful to my God or this world if I am self absorbed.

Prayer for the day

I pray to be useful to others through my God. I pray for the removal of self that I can better do the will of my Higher Power. Self cannot overcome self, so I will pray for Divine assistance to lead me to freedom.

Mantra for the day

I seek to be useful and free from the bondage of self. I seek to be useful and free from the bondage of self. I seek to be useful and free from the bondage of self.

Reflection for the day

_____

_____

_____

_____

_____

_____

_____

_____

_____

_____

_____

_____

_____

_____

_____

_____

Thought for the day

I am more than the sum of my body parts. I am pleased that my sexuality is mine to control, while many males are controlled by their sexual desires. It pleases me that men look to me for fulfillment, unfortunately their eye is skewed. Men see parts of me, but they fail to see the whole of me. I am much more than most males will ever realize. It takes a strong, powerful woman to broaden their horizons sufficient to fulfill them. It takes intellect and a calm, helpful heart to give them the guidance they need to be given the ability to see the total worth of an enlightened woman.

Meditation for the day

I am aware of opportunities to be useful to the males in my life. I seek to redirect their energies so they too can find peace and satisfaction in themselves and not in their selfish conquests. Eventually women will unite in this effort to confront this deficiency in male perception. Together we are strong.

Prayer for the day

I pray for the strength and wisdom to use my sensuality for the betterment of men. I ask that I may see myself as a holistic, helpful person with the strength of character to guide men to a better understanding of themselves, and promote their usefulness to womankind.

Mantra for the day

I will celebrate my whole being. I will celebrate my whole being. I will celebrate my whole being.

Reflection for the day

_____

_____

_____

_____

_____

_____

_____

_____

_____

_____

_____

_____

_____

_____

_____

_____

_____

_____

Thought for the day

I've turned my will and my life over to the care of God. I am no longer powerless over life and its troubles. Today, through my decision and my actions I am empowered to be the strong, intelligent and kind woman my Creator designed me to be. I use my spiritual advantage to promote and care for those who have distanced themselves from the love of the Spirit. I trust that the power of God flowing through me will motivate those less fortunate to follow me back to their Source of strength. God has given me the power to lead the lost home. I relish this…the greatest of all gifts.

Meditation for the day

Today, I am grateful for the spiritual advantage that I've been blessed with. I use this advantage to promote the love that our Creator has so unselfishly bestowed upon me. My sisters will be lifted with love. Men will be made ready for a spiritual transformation that will enable them to be of use to women. Men need to exalt me as I exalt my God. Men need to serve me as I serve the Divine if they want to feel the freedom and joy that I cherish. I earn my freedom through service to my God this service gives me my spiritual advantage that enables me to help others.

Prayer for the day

I pray that I am forever grateful for the spiritual advantage with which I have been blessed. I pray that I can unselfishly use my gifts to raise my sisters, and ready males for their spiritual journey; transformed and forever changed to view and treat women as the goddesses that they are. I pray that all women will unite and claim the power that is rightfully ours.

Mantra for the day

I am power, I am love, I am of service. I am power, I am love, I am of service. I am power, I am love, I am of service.

Reflection for the day

_____

_____

_____

_____

_____

_____

_____

_____

_____

_____

_____

_____

_____

_____

_____

_____

Thought for the day

Disappointments, sorrow, pain and loss are not mine. These are worldly items that I no longer lay claim to. With Divine assistance I have distanced myself from my past life. I have been reborn. I have been born into a new and wonderful world free from fear, petty hardships, and spiritual discord. Women love me and men adore me. I have become what I have always sought. Self-confidence and emotional stability bring people to me for the love I offer. It pleases my God to be of use to all children of Spirit. Free from the common; I have become useful.

Meditation for the day

Love is only love when it flows freely. It is my privilege to let God's grace and power flow through me so that others can be aware of the Divine light. I am sustained by this free flow of spiritual energy. It is not mine to keep. I am a small part of the Circle of Life.

Prayer for the day

I pray for the grace to maintain my spiritual distance from the world. I ask to live in a realistic life of love and compassion. I pray for the grace to fortify myself from evil and spread the love of the Divine. I pray for the Power to do good works.

Mantra for the day

I am God's love in action. I am God's love in action. I am God's love in action.

Reflection for the day

_____

_____

_____

_____

_____

_____

_____

_____

_____

_____

_____

_____

_____

_____

_____

_____

Thought for the day

Our society often teaches young girls to
view other girls as the enemy. We therefore grow
up in an unhealthy competition with other women
feeling threatened by their self-confidence, strength
and beauty. It is time to let all of that go. We need
to celebrate and encourage these virtues in each
other. Know that we each have special gifts and
talents that enrich the lives of others around us and
begin to celebrate the wonderful creatures we are
and are continuing to become.

Meditation for the day

Today I focus on the gifts of the women in
my life. I learn to incorporate the knowledge I gain
from them into my own life and seek to add to
theirs. I continue to offer encouragement and
strength so as to better all of our lives.

Prayer for the day

I pray for knowledge to share with other
women. I request to present myself in a way that
shows courage and compassion. I pray to let go of
falsehoods pushed on me by a society that seeks to
isolate women as a means to keep them in a
subservient role.

Mantra for the day

I am woman, hear me roar; in numbers too big to ignore. I am woman hear me roar; in numbers too big to ignore.

Reflection for the day

_____

_____

_____

_____

_____

_____

_____

_____

_____

_____

_____

_____

_____

_____

Thought for the day

Our sense of self develops with experiences, perceptions and time. How we see ourselves as young children, adolescents, young adults, or middle age will all be different at the differing stages. This is due to the variety of contributing factors that occur in our life. What can we do if our sense of self is underdeveloped or if our view is skewed? Since we cannot change our experiences or time, we sometimes need to look at our perception of things. Some experiences may have taught us that we are not in control of our emotions, or it could be we have learned to see ourselves as less than. Today I realize that I do have the inner strength to ascend toward my true potential. I can view the effects of my experiences differently and focus on the strengths instead of the weaknesses.

Meditation for the day

Today I examine my current status in life. I turn my thoughts toward my perceived strengths instead of allowing the shortcomings to be my view.

Prayer for the day

I ask for continued strength to face today. I pray for courage to address troubling issues if they arise and wisdom to prevent me from straying from the now. I ask for presence of mind to recognize my strengths and pass them along to others.

Mantra for the day

I focus my thoughts on current strengths knowing I am always blessed. I focus my thoughts on current strengths knowing I am always blessed.

Reflection for the day

_____

_____

_____

_____

_____

_____

_____

_____

_____

_____

_____

_____

_____

_____

_____

_____

Thought for the day

I heard a woman speaker once talk of her relationships. She said something very profound and it bears repeating. 'In all my relationships, I was given things that man made: money, jewels, clothing, homes. What was expected in return is of far greater value, something made by God.' We are the gift, God's greatest creation. This is one of the most valuable bits of knowledge we can possess. Yet, we often have traded this treasure for trash with an end result of personal and emotional distress leading to heartache. Our sense of self needs to be such that this treasure is guarded sacredly as the gift it is. When I devalue myself by carelessly and aimlessly trading what I possess for wanton "goods", I devalue my relationship with myself and my Maker. Our worth is so much more.

Meditation for the day

I look within at the treasure with which I am blessed. My center is focused on building a relationship with myself that allows me to make rational but heartfelt decisions regarding with whom I choose to share my treasure. The strength I have will be used wisely to make decisions that affect my view of myself.

Prayer for the day

I pray for discernment in making the weighty decisions of sharing myself with others. I ask that in making these decisions I will honor myself as well as women in my life. With gratitude for my gifts, I strive to make choices that are worthy of those blessings.

Mantra for the day

I am fearfully and wonderfully made. I am fearfully and wonderfully made. I am fearfully and wonderfully made.

Reflection for the day

_____

_____

_____

_____

_____

_____

_____

_____

_____

_____

_____

_____

_____

_____

_____

_____

_____

_____

Thought for the Day

The rooster crows, but the hen delivers! (Sorry but I just couldn't help myself!) It does sound vaguely familiar though. I have seen my share of chest-beaters and glory-seekers. While these folks are going about their self-centered lives, women are quietly getting things done. We don't seem to get much credit for sitting up all night with a sick child. No one offers to help as we do soiled laundry and clean up vomit. No pat on the back for explaining to a grieving child why their beloved pet has died. There doesn't seem to be much glory in being female. That's probably because we don't have the time or the inclination to seek it. We just strive to do all the unseen and dirty little jobs that make us gloriously happy and fulfilled.

Meditation for the day

I consider what really brings my peace and fulfillment. In addition to family and career, I take time to love all the people that I can. I have a smile whether I am tired or not. I have time to listen with a helpful heart to a friend in need. I have the time and the energy to be a woman of love.

Prayer for the Day

I pray to remain joyous and fulfilled by the opportunities of life. What some may consider trite, I build a life of happiness and fulfillment on. This is the freedom that I have always sought; to place value on the important events in my life.

Mantra for the day

Let the roosters crow, I have a life to live. ☺

Reflection for the day

_____

_____

_____

_____

_____

_____

_____

_____

_____

_____

_____

_____

_____

_____

_____

_____

_____

Thought for the day

No man is good enough to govern a woman without her consent. -- Susan B. Anthony

Consent seems to be the key word here. For a variety of reasons, often unhealthy, some women seek an overbearing man to come into their lives and rescue them. This book is designed to touch just the opposite. We must celebrate the strength of women and the independent man that seek to willingly consent to female leadership. It is socially acceptable to be a strong woman, but to be a submissive male in this society takes a great deal of inner strength. A man that can fully love, fully trust and fully give himself to the beauty of love is a rare man of great strength and wisdom. These men are currently celebrating female advantage and will be there as society adopts the inevitable change to the feminine values of love and peace. What often looks like a 'henpecked' man is doing his part to create a new and vital social construct designed to change the world. He has willingly given consent to change himself and the world through the celebration of the female.

Meditation for the Day

I will consider the strength of a man that willingly gives his all to the woman he loves and womankind in general. I will applaud his unselfish devotion to female leadership and his desire to lead other men by example. Women can change the world by themselves. However, the example a loving helpmate will enable women and men to bond together to promote the changes in society that we desire.

Prayer for the Day

Today I can rightly gives thanks to the more enlightened men who work for the betterment of the world. I ask that I be given a pure heart and motive so that I can graciously receive their offerings. I seek to fully understand the value of a well-intentioned man of character.

Mantra for the Day

We can work together for greater change. We can work together for greater change. We can work together for greater change.

Reflection for the day

_____

_____

_____

_____

_____

_____

_____

_____

_____

_____

_____

Thought for the Day

We have all heard it, 'change takes time'.
That statement is true, but if we wait for the time to
change, it will never happen. Some of us have said
I am a very busy woman and I want a new life but I
don't have the time or the energy to promote
myself. We can all begin today to build the new life
that we seek. When I brush my hair in the morning,
I can look in the mirror, reaffirm my belief in
myself and set one small positive goal for my day.
Big change is accomplished by a series of small
positive actions that, when connected, propel us to
the new life that we seek. It sometimes feels like I
have a world full of people trying to drain me of
time and energy. The new me will find balance in
these matters by placing my needs and my welfare
first. I cannot be beneficial to anyone if I am
depleted. I will make the time to change.

Meditation for the Day

Today I realize that if I do not honor myself
and care for myself no one else will either. I have
varied responsibilities that all begin with me. On
this day I reflect on how to properly care for myself
and work for a brighter tomorrow.

Prayer for the Day

As I communicate with my Creator, I will
ask to be guilt free in my requests for time to build a
better future. I need always remember that as I
grow, so will those I love. As a leader, I must go
first. I humbly ask that the quality of life to which I
aspire will be a blessing for all.

Mantra for the Day

I have the time to change. I have the time to change. I have the time to change.

Reflection for the day

_____

_____

_____

_____

_____

_____

_____

_____

_____

_____

_____

_____

_____

_____

_____

_____

_____

Thought for the day

As we search for our individual power, we shall understand that the power comes from within. The power we have is to be used wisely and not to be used to manipulate people. We are trying to improve relationships through love, patience, tolerance, and a new spirit. If we try to manipulate instead of lead those we love, we are most likely to encounter resistance. Our rise to self-awareness and responsibility is intended to encourage and enhance unity, not division. We can all feel the difference between thoughtful leadership and manipulation. Let us be conscientious in our efforts to promote peaceful union. As an enlightened woman, I seek peace in all of my relationships.

Meditation for the day

I ponder what styles of leadership that I find most attractive. I'm most drawn to intelligent, well-thought out ideas that are adequately explained and supported. I do not respond well to over-bearing, egotistical power drives, and I will not lower myself to these standards. As an enlightened woman, I will guide with love, emotional stability, and support. I will share what best works for me.

Prayer for the day

I ask for a balanced approach in my personal relationships. I pray to be free from selfishness and accept the role of guide for the greater good of all. I shall remain humble in my efforts to lead with a firm and fair hand.

Mantra for the day

Attractive leaders attract. Attractive leaders attract. Attractive leaders attract.

Reflection for the day

_____

_____

_____

_____

_____

_____

_____

_____

_____

_____

_____

_____

_____

_____

_____

_____

_____

_____

Thought for the day

Sometimes we get flawed information. It seems throughout my life, when seeking comfort for romantic difficulties I have been advised to follow my heart. That does sound romantic, but it appears to be a failed philosophy. Today I find advantage in leading with my heart. I realize that my loving God has given me intellect to use. The powerful combination of intellect, experience and stable emotions will allow my heart to lead me in the proper direction. I need always remember that my emotions are subject to my will and not the other way around. My mind and my heart are united to create a better, more peaceful and meaningful life. My new life demands that I be proactive and no longer reactive, I lead my life and I follow no one.

Meditation for the Day

I am no longer a passive woman playing catch up in this life. I can now use my heart with assurance for it has been fortified with Power and goodness. When I lead with my heart, I bring the love of my Creator into all situations. When I followed my heart, I walked alone. I am a leader for my heart is full and does not want.

Prayer for the Day

I ask for the insight and the strength to live the life I want. It is my desire to have my heart ever strengthened and fortified by Divine love. This real and true love will give me all I need to lead with assurance and to transcend the difficulties of life and love.

Mantra for the Day

I no longer follow my heart, I lead with it. I no longer follow my heart, I lead with it. I no longer follow my heart, I lead with it.

Reflection for the day

_____

_____

_____

_____

_____

_____

_____

_____

_____

_____

_____

_____

_____

_____

_____

Thought for the Day

The desire for power and control is what continues to separate the sexes. When all parties concerned decide on the proper placement of their energies there will be peace in the home. For the empowered woman it is easy to claim her place as head of the house. Both she and her mate realize that she is the strength in the family and he is the appreciated and well-loved helpmate. When the issue of power is resolved, the issue of separation will be resolved. I claim my place as head of the household to provide peace and comfort for all. I desire a peaceful, loving home and I am willing to work for it.

Meditation for the Day

I take the time to realize my true place in my relationship. How many times has he asked me to make the decisions? If I listen closely to my mate, I will hear his desire for me to take the lead. A well-informed man seeks a strong woman to follow for he knows he will excel in a peaceful environment.

Prayer for the Day

I ask that I be given the insight to recognize and claim my true power as head of the household. I pray for a peaceful and fulfilled heart as I make the changes that will most benefit those that I love. I fear not, for I am filled with the Spirit.

Mantra for the Day

I provide peace and comfort. I provide peace and comfort. I provide peace and comfort.

Reflection for the day

_____

_____

_____

_____

_____

_____

_____

_____

_____

_____

_____

_____

_____

_____

_____

_____

Thought for the day

**I would rather have a mind opened by wonder than one
closed by belief. -- Gary Spence**

Before I started my journey toward a new
life, I was fettered by the beliefs of my past. I
viewed the world and people with fixed ideas that
continued to deter my progress. Then one day when
perplexed by my limited growth, I began to wonder
and my mind opened. I wondered what I could be, I
wondered what I could do, and most importantly, I
wondered if my beliefs could change. My wonder
changed to curiosity, my curiosity changed to
question, my question led to action and my actions
created not only a new belief, but a new faith as
well. Today my wonder is an open mind that can
create all of the possibilities that I seek.

Meditation for the Day

Belief is everything. I need to question my
beliefs on a regular basis if I expect to continue my
transformation to enlightenment. My new beliefs
are motivated by an open mind and a desire for
continued growth. No longer will my beliefs be
based in convenience or the approval of others. My
mind is free to wonder, ever searching for a better
life.

Prayer for the Day

I seek to keep the wonder of a child. I ask
the Power to remain humble and pliant in my
beliefs and actions. My Creator has given me the
gift of wonder. I will not squander the gift.

Mantra for the Day

To wonder is wonderful! To wonder is wonderful! To wonder is wonderful!

Reflection for the day

_____

_____

_____

_____

_____

_____

_____

_____

_____

_____

_____

_____

_____

_____

_____

_____

_____

Thought for the day

Voices from the past can haunt us. It's as if a sad yet familiar song replays in our mind ready to curtail our progression. "You big dummy, what's wrong with you anyway?" "Are you stupid or just lazy?" You can only hear this so many times before you begin to believe it. Somehow, it permeates your soul and causes you to deny your spirit the love and reverence so richly deserved. As a spiritual being, it is imperative that we cultivate and exhilarate our sacred vital force. We have the power to change the song. Change it to one of beauty, high-hearted love. Write yourself a new love song.

Meditation for the day

Today I will examine the messages I hear so I can begin to change them. I look to the spiritual principles I possess to provide direction that will allow the truth of the day to outcry the harsh and hurtful voices of the past.

Prayer for the day

I ask to learn to listen to the real truth within. I pray for the fortitude and presence of mind to recognize the lies from my past that so diminish my spirit. I desire wisdom to replace these malignant voices from the past with prodigious and independent mettle.

Mantra for the day

I am hearing a new song today. It is a song of incredible love. I am hearing a new song today. It is a song of incredible love.

Reflection for the day

_____

_____

_____

_____

_____

_____

_____

_____

_____

_____

_____

_____

_____

_____

_____

_____

Thought for the day

I am enough! I need always remember that I have been created in the image of God. I am powerful, capable, and worthy. I used to present an image of uncertainty, weakness, and fragility. This image not only hurt me professionally it also unknowingly invited predators into my life. I felt that everything and everyone were my enemies. Once again my greatest enemy was my lack of self-worth, which opened the door for negative energy to overwhelm me. I now realize that I was a queen my whole life and I had latent power at my hand. I seek my power, I claim my power, I am goodness and strength. Today the predators are gone. Predators attack the weak and the weak-willed. I am no longer filled with the weakness of fear. I am fortified with faith. Today the wild beasts of life flee from the strength I posses and the goodness that I share.

Meditation for the day

I refuse to engage in negativity. An enlightened queen does not entertain nefarious thoughts or actions. My realm is filled with goodness and kindness. I am light, I am power, and the predators of life flee from me.

Prayer for the day

I pray that I may fully engage my power and strength. I pray that the predators be transformed into pawns. Let them be humbled and made useful. Only in this way will they transform their darkness into light and be made whole at last.

Mantra for the day

My strength negates all predatory actions. My strength negates all predatory actions. My strength negates all predatory actions.

Reflection for the day

_____

_____

_____

_____

_____

_____

_____

_____

_____

_____

_____

_____

_____

_____

_____

_____

Thought for the day

Where do I go from here? Well, there is nowhere to go, you are already there. Here, there, whatever you want to call it is not a destination. It is usually a way we define our dissatisfaction with the present. We want to "go" instead of working to change our perceptions. When our life is spirit-centered there is no place to go, only work to be done. Work to better our understanding and relationship with our Creator. Work to improve our ever growing intimate relationships with our empowered female friends. Work to further the leading of males so they too can find satisfaction in their place and rise to their potential and a new understanding of life.

Meditation for the day

I'm not going to be okay. I'm not going to be fine, I already posses these qualities for I am whole today. This is the day I'm working on. It is sufficient unto itself, and so am I!

Prayer for the day

I pray that I can internalize the fact that *I am* sufficient for this day. No one can interfere with my satisfaction with self. No one can bring me down. The Power runs deep through my soul and is not concerned or bothered by worldly matters.

Mantra for the day

     I have arrived and God and I are enough for this day. I have arrived and God and I are enough for this day. I have arrived and God and I are enough for this day.

Reflection for the day

_____

_____

_____

_____

_____

_____

_____

_____

_____

_____

_____

_____

_____

_____

_____

Thought for the day

Change! There are so many things to change in life, but the hardest seem to be our responses to those actions witnessed as a child. Those old role models were great for the times but times change. Women are no longer expected to willingly submit at home or in the work place; yet the old tapes remain. You remember what they said; don't rock the boat, do not challenge male authority, be a good girl, people will talk. Well, it is a new day! I will rock the boat, I'm as good as I WANT to be, let them talk, and isn't male authority an oxymoron? The only person that is going to change my perceptions of life is me. I choose to believe different, I choose to act different, I choose to interact with others differently and I expect different results. Today I do not await my fate, I seek to fulfill my goals, and have others meet my expectations. I am a queen and a creator.

Meditation for the day

Why would a new woman choose to live in an old world? I am a new woman and I will create a new world. My world, a world that is safe, appealing and satisfying to my wants, needs and desires. Sisters nourish, men provide, I am satisfied with my new world.

Prayer for the day

I pray for the tenacity to create a new world for myself and others. I pray to do this through new actions, thoughts and deeds. God, the people that love me and I can, and will build a better world. This will be a new and more enriching world that I can live in freely and with contentment.

Mantra for the day

I am a new woman with my new world. I am a new woman with my new world. I am a new woman with my new world.

Reflection for the day

_____

_____

_____

_____

_____

_____

_____

_____

_____

_____

_____

_____

_____

_____

_____

_____

_____

Thought for the day

      The female training of men. This does sound a little harsh doesn't it? Why would a woman want to change a man? The answer is simply so he can grow spiritually, become a better man and be more useful to her. Many men learn about life on the playground, intimacy (sex) is taught in the locker room and all talk of emotional well being is avoided at all costs. What we call feelings are avoided or easily dismissed by men as being unnecessary. For many men their emotions are limited to only the basics of lust and rage. These two emotions pretty well define selfishness. Lust says I want to, rage says I'm not going to. This is the depiction of the primitive mind of a man that has not been helped to see the grander glory of female enlightenment. If, as women, we really desire to change the world for the better, we must reach behind us to help a male who still suffers in ignorance and lead him to the greater good that lies deep within him.

Meditation for the day

      Today I take time out of my life to try to help a man. I feel it is in everyone's best interest for men to evolve as woman has. I no longer tolerate primitive, rude behavior from a male. I will open my heart to the men I love and lead them to a new understanding.

Prayer for the day

      I pray for power, strength and wisdom to offer loving guidance and renewal. I ask to be sincere and humble in my approach so as to provide needed leadership toward the betterment of all.

Mantra for the day

My kindness and love can change the world. My kindness and love can change the world. My kindness and love can change the world.

Reflection for the day

_____

_____

_____

_____

_____

_____

_____

_____

_____

_____

_____

_____

_____

_____

_____

_____

_____

_____

_____

Thought for the day

My spirit needs loving attention too. I need to evermore increase my awareness and connection to my God. Through prayer and meditation I come to know who I really am. As God reveals a new understanding of me I stand in awe and wonder. Calmness and peace are mine to claim. How could I come this far without the spiritual connection that I now enjoy? How and why did I think I could have a meaningful life without the development of my best asset? I am my Spirit; it defines me. I am at peace with this wonderful part of me. From my spirit come my feistiness and my peace. I am willing to continue my spiritual growth. As I grow spiritually I will be able to bring peace, joy and proper direction to those in my life. My Spirit will help me to be helpful.

Meditation for the day

I continue my spiritual growth. I honor my God by being the best spirit that I can be. I remove my selfish thoughts and think of how I can best positively contribute to the world. I meditate on a joyous heart and a quiet mind. I am the best of the Best. I grow in the image of my God. This spiritual growth pleases both God and me for I am useful at last!

Prayer for the day

I pray to give God the time it takes to mold me into the woman I've always wanted to be. I pray to live the life of a goddess. I want so very much to be kindness and Spirit in action. It is my desire for all to see the smile of God in my actions, and to feel Divine Love through me.

Mantra for the day

I am the Spirit of goodness. I am the Spirit of goodness. I am the Spirit of goodness.

Reflection for the day

_____

_____

_____

_____

_____

_____

_____

_____

_____

_____

_____

_____

_____

_____

_____

_____

_____

_____

113

Thought for the day
   Once upon a time! My, oh my,
the time I've wasted on these youthful fantasies! It
really is not our fault we were fed this concept of
life since conception. Today I can honestly say I'm
happy these falsehoods did not impose themselves
on my life. When I decided that my life was my
responsibility, I moved from fantasy to reality.
There is no substitute for hard work and
independent fortitude. No one can honestly bring
me the satisfaction that I seek. I set the standards
for myself and I decide when I've been a success.
This is the only true path to freedom. My reliance
on others for my place in life will keep me
insufficient unto myself and continue to promote
the negativity that I've found so detrimental to my
rise as ruler of my realm.

Meditation for the day
   No need to ponder the time wasted trying to
meet the ideals of others. No need to see the folly
of foisted emotions in past relationships. Today I
live in reality. I meet my standards, and I deal in
the beauty and reality of life. No elusive fantasy
can match the reality of my ascent to fulfillment.
Success and freedom are mine; I've worked for
them, I claim them.

Prayer for the day
   I pray for the ability to see the truth as it is
and to work for positive changes to benefit myself
and others. I pray to move ever further from the
fantasy of childhood, and to claim my reality as a
mature woman of faith.

Mantra for the day

I provide the freedom that I seek. I provide the freedom that I seek. I provide the freedom that I seek.

Reflection for the day

_____

_____

_____

_____

_____

_____

_____

_____

_____

_____

_____

_____

_____

_____

_____

_____

_____

Thought for the day

Thought for the day? Do we really take the time to think? Most of my life has been a reactionary existence. It seems that I was always responding to someone else's thoughts and actions. By living on the backside of life I never gave myself the necessary time to grow and enhance my intellectual and emotional capabilities. I was much too busy trying to please rather than being pleased. The woman I am today is not reactive, but proactive. I take the time to read, pray and discuss with others to gain new and helpful insight to life. I will find quiet, self-reflective times to fully develop my ideas before I express them. As a leader it is my responsibility to bring only the best, most sound thoughts and ideas to those around me. A leader is calm, introspective, intelligent and kind.

Meditation for the day

Today I meditate on my strengths. I reflect on the squandered time spent reacting to others. I seek to enhance my thought processes and give myself full credit for my intellectual capabilities. The goodness of my heart will work in concert with my virtuous mind to bring forth the best plan of action for those who love me.

Prayer for the day

I pray to always give God time in the formulation of thought, word and deed. I need Divine assistance to enable me to be a more effective and gracious leader. I pray to develop true leadership skills and not slip into the tyranny that was imposed on me.

Mantra for the day

I am a benevolent leader, I am proactive. I am a benevolent leader, I am proactive. I am a benevolent leader, I am proactive.

Reflection for the day

_____

_____

_____

_____

_____

_____

_____

_____

_____

_____

_____

_____

_____

_____

_____

_____

Thought for the day

Wow! Oh look, it is a brand new day! That means that I have all choices available to me once more. What will I decide to do with this day? When we become active and not passive in our life we are given a fresh start each and every day. Even if throughout the day our circumstances are unlikely to change, I can change my perceptions of people and events that will enable me to bring peace to any situation. The world and my life are mine to command when I accept the challenge to be a leader and not a passive participant. Leaders promote change in themselves, others, and the world. Passive people reluctantly settle for what they get. When I'm tired of taking the scraps that this life throws me, I stand up and claim my power as a proactive participant in life. It is a brand new day!

Meditation for the day

Today I question from where my reluctance to lead comes. Is this resistance left over from the past, or do current situations and people stifle my growth? I need to find the answers to these questions then seek out the help that enables me to be free to grow into the strong, purposeful woman that I have always dreamed of being.

Prayer for the day

I pray for the strength to meet and to overcome my resistance to change. I pray that my God gives me the strength that I need to meet this new day and to grasp the new opportunities that it presents.

Mantra for the day

      I am a new woman for this new day. I am a new woman for this new day. I am a new woman for this new day.

Reflection for the day

_____

_____

_____

_____

_____

_____

_____

_____

_____

_____

_____

_____

_____

_____

_____

_____

Thought for the day

The changes that I seek will not immediately bring me comfort. I do not change by being comfortable or doing what I want. If I am to alter my thoughts, perceptions and position in life, it will require a painful examination of my beliefs. It is always uncomfortable to give up the familiar (even if it doesn't work) for the new and untested. What happens is that as we are making progress, our faith will waver and we fall back into the old, unproductive familiar that we are attempting to change. It is important to realize that pain and uncertainty will be a part of my journey to a new and more productive life. I can learn from, and lean on the sisters that have gone before me. Faith in God and the sisterhood will sustain me during my trials.

Meditation for the day

I reflect on the progress I have made in life. What I see is that lasting change has often come slowly and with an element of pain and uncertainty. I need not fear change. I need only to faithfully embrace it. My new life is going to be much better than the former. I need not fear the future for it is mine to command.

Prayer for the day

I ask for the confidence and patience to pursue my dreams. I strive to be the queen that my God has destined me to be. The discomfort of change cannot dampen the spirit of a determined woman. I use my faith to lean on the sisters while I reach back for those to come. Together we are strong and we fear not the challenge of change.

Mantra for the day

I have all the support that I need. I have all the support that I need. I have all the support that I need.

Reflection for the day

_____

_____

_____

_____

_____

_____

_____

_____

_____

_____

_____

_____

_____

_____

_____

_____

_____

_____

Thought for the day

NO. The word no is a complete sentence.
When children are in their 'terrible-twos', we hear
the word no a lot. Psychologically speaking, this is
where the child is seeking autonomy. This is their
effort to define themselves independently of their
parents. The child that just wanted to play and be
comforted now strikes out on their own to discover
the new world they are living in. These two year
olds soon find that the world is exciting, frightening
and fun. Whenever someone tries to impede the
child's curiosity or growth they unapologetically
scream 'no'. Now I, once again, find myself
wanting to make a break from the restraints that
slow my personal progress and hinder my freedom.
Only this time I am strangely burdened with guilt. I
wonder why I often feel the need to apologize for
saying 'no'. I wonder why I often need to explain
myself when I say 'no'.

Meditation for the day

Why did I let 'them' take my right to freely
say 'no'? How often have I given in to stronger
voices, how often have I kowtowed when my heart
and mind knew better? I experience my new world
without the impediment of others. I claim my
freedom to explore and learn on my terms. Part of
my growth as an independent, free thinking woman
is to once again learn how to guiltlessly say 'no'.
Today I will reclaim my right to say no with
impunity.

Prayer for the day

I pray for the power to say 'no'. I say no
without comment or justification. I pray to stay
strong in my one word sentence. 'No'.

Mantra for the day

It's ok to say 'no'. It's ok to say 'no'. It's ok to say 'no'.

Reflection for the day

_____

_____

_____

_____

_____

_____

_____

_____

_____

_____

_____

_____

_____

_____

_____

_____

_____

Thought for the day

It would seem that women are born and socialized to give and receive love. Men, on the other hand, seem to have been shortchanged. Most males can receive love on a limited basis but they have great difficulty in giving and sharing the greatest gift of all. A wise woman knows that she must teach her man how to love. She must teach him the fine art of intimacy and sharing from the heart. Without the efforts of strong, intelligent women to provide the safety that he needs, most men will simply never learn how to be a good partner. The woman is the gift. Part of the gift she shares is to teach others how to come out of hiding and to learn the benefits of love. A well-informed queen can strip the male of his defenses and leave him emotionally free to experience and grow in the love that is pleasing for all.

Meditation for the day

I realize that the perfect partner is not out there for me. I also realize that I have been given the strength and power of love. I use my gift to create that for which I have searched in vain. Why would I want a man 'off of the rack' when I can be the 'designer' and get what really pleases me? I'll take the time and the effort to create a pleasing male.

Prayer for the day

I pray to overcome the effects of the emotionally safe and good girl that I was socialized to be. Today, I have the strength, intelligence and heart to get what I seek. I pray to never settle for an emotionally distant male. I ask for the perseverance to remain strong as I teach him how to be beneficial to me.

Mantra for the day
    I will communicate my desires. I will communicate my desires. I will communicate my desires.

Reflection for the day

_____

_____

_____

_____

_____

_____

_____

_____

_____

_____

_____

_____

_____

_____

_____

_____

Thought for the day

It is really not their fault. Men are socialized to be strong and fearless. They are also taught to be protective (controlling?) of women. For this to happen they develop a whole arsenal of defenses that enable them to not feel the same emotions that we do. When a woman becomes powerful and self-assured the man no longer sees a need to be protective of her. If she can make him feel safe and loved while maintaining her independence, his walls will slowly come down. When he can feel safe under her guidance, he can free himself from the restraints that society has placed on him. The male need for freedom is best achieved under female guidance. His first authority figure was female, and he feels comforted by a strong capable woman. Much like us, when a man enters his comfort zone he too will grow.

Meditation for the day

I will contemplate how best to bring the men in my life peace by becoming a more capable, independent, and compassionate woman. As I grow in my independence I will realize that my new self-confidence will be a comfort to those that I love. They will feel more at peace for they will know I live safely and confidently under the ever-watchful eye of my loving God.

Prayer for the day

I pray that my new strength and independence will enhance the lives of those who surround me. As I focus on my own growth those that love me will be free from old patriarchal dictates; this liberation will open the path for their own personal development. I pray that as we grow separately, we too will grow in love together.

Mantra for the day
 My actions provide comfort. My actions provide comfort. My actions provide comfort.

Reflection for the day

_____

_____

_____

_____

_____

_____

_____

_____

_____

_____

_____

_____

_____

_____

Thought for the day

It saddens me to think of the time wasted seeking the approval of others. Whether it is an overbearing parent, a controlling boyfriend or husband, or a demanding employer we will stifle our own welfare in direct proportion to our efforts to satisfy them. Trying to be something or someone I'm not is a huge waste of time, effort, and dignity. When we move away from the perceived perfection they want, we begin to see ourselves for who we truly are. We are real with real problems, real shortcomings and a real sincere desire to please ourselves. I need to consult with my God and together we will chart a path that leads to my personal fulfillment. I am enough. I do not need and I do not seek another's approval to validate myself. I will not stifle my own growth for another's approval or enjoyment.

Meditation for the day

Today I consider how best to meet my needs and to fulfill my desires. I do not have any time or energy to contemplate the approval of others. Living within the guidelines of my own spiritual principles provides for my own approval and ultimately my own satisfaction. I will not trade my spiritual satisfaction for the mean-spirited desires of a mortal.

Prayer for the day

Today I ask for the willingness and fortitude to meet my spiritual goals and objectives. When I am satisfied spiritually most people will view me as an example and not a project.

Mantra for the day

I am willing to grow to my standards. I am willing to grow to my standards. I am willing to grow to my standards.

Reflection for the day

_____

_____

_____

_____

_____

_____

_____

_____

_____

_____

_____

_____

_____

_____

_____

_____

_____

_____

Thought for the day
    The days of being passive are over. One of
the main contributing factors to my passivity was
lack of purpose. I had not yet realized my own
personal worth. I had not yet decided to claim my
place as a queen. My passivity was born of
convenience not of conviction. I had no real desire
to give in, no desire to submit, but I also had no
sincere desire to fight for my own welfare. I was in
emotional limbo, floating from one insufficient
cause to another. I had no passion or conviction to
seek my own inner goddess. I need to get excited
about my life and the passionate possibilities that it
holds. I need to be firm in my convictions that I am
worthy of worship and adoration. When I lack
passionate cause and conviction, I open myself to
the predators of the world. As I define myself, set
an agenda for my life and seek to satisfy the queen
within, my passivity falls by the wayside and a new
self-assured, passionate woman is born

Meditation for the day
    I will reflect on the causes of my passivity.
Some contributing factors might be voices from the
past, not too distant verbal abuse and humiliation, or
lack of drive and purpose. As I am able to recognize
the causes of my problems it will become
abundantly clear that these issues are not life-long
impediments to my growth as a queen. My personal
freedom and direction are ALWAYS mine to claim.

Prayer for the day
    I pray to replace my former passivity with
proper assertiveness. I pray for guidance and
strength so I do not waver in my new convictions to
seek my true worth. I pray to be the first to know

and believe that I am an enlightened and powerful woman.

Mantra for the day
   My passivity is passé. My passivity is passé. My passivity is passé.

Reflection for the day

_____

_____

_____

_____

_____

_____

_____

_____

_____

_____

_____

_____

_____

_____

_____

_____

Thought for the day

Just think what it would be like to have a knowledgeable, kind and passionate partner that cared for our feelings yet surrendered to our wishes. The world is full of submissive men. This is probably one of the best kept secrets of our time. These men are not weak, they are not failures, and they are quite capable of competing in a 'man's' world. However, they long to treat a woman as the queen that she is. Their world is a world of service to their queen and goddess. Their hearts fill when she is happy and her needs are met. They clean house, wait on you hand and foot, give massages and pedicures. Additionally, they share thoughtful opinions when asked and submit to your final decision. These are men that are unseen in the community and secretly dream of a queen to serve fully and completely. Their dreams are often unfulfilled because many women lack the understanding that it takes to claim their rightful place as a queen and allow a male into her service. This is the type of service and woman for which he has waited a lifetime. There are far too many women still seeking partnership instead of leadership.

Meditation for the day

I've heard more than one woman say 'what I really need is a wife'. Of course they are referring to the old sexist roles from which we women are trying to break free. Whether we are stay-at-home moms or executives, it is easy to see the benefits of coming home to a clean house and a well-cooked meal. I should be free to relax or work after dinner while he cleans the dishes and tends to my needs. I will meditate on the possibilities of taking a leadership role. I look at the successful couples I know. Someone is usually in a leadership role, why shouldn't it be me?

Prayer for the day

I pray for an open mind. I examine my beliefs and see if I am truly ready to move from patriarchy to matriarchy.

Mantra for the day

There is no parity, I can either lead or follow. There is no parity, I can either lead or follow. There is no parity, I can either lead or follow.

Reflection for the day

_____

_____

_____

_____

_____

_____

_____

_____

_____

_____

_____

_____

Thought for the day

When we diminish others, we diminish ourselves. How often do we point out the flaws of others only to find ourselves questioning similar things in our appearance, demeanor, relationships, etc.? We can only learn to appreciate ourselves with a sense of awe when we do the same for others. "Look at the strength she has," "What a beautiful smile and sparkle in her eyes." These are what we need to say instead of pointing out someone's weaknesses. We all possess both, let's focus on the good and beautiful in each other and therefore enrich both of our lives.

Meditation for the day

Instead of looking at what's wrong, I will focus on what is right. I refuse to diminish others and subsequently myself. I can strengthen others as well as myself by doing what is kind and loving instead of diminishing and punishing.

Prayer for the day

I pray for a kind heart. I pray to display the same kind regard for others that I would have shown to me. I ask for the strength to reach out and be that thoughtful person today in order to enrich my life as well as others.

Mantra for the day

I am strong enough to show the kind regard that others' deserve. I will learn to accept that from others as well. I am strong enough to show the kind regard that others' deserve.

Reflection for the day

_____

_____

_____

_____

_____

_____

_____

_____

_____

_____

_____

_____

_____

_____

_____

Thought for the day

In my work, I often see women that have been emotionally raped. They have had their dignity, their personhood, their femininity taken from them by force. I have learned in my personal growth that emotional pain can be repaired. It definitely takes work, but it is well worth the effort. First, I had to recognize what had taken place and deal with the resulting resentment and depression that followed. Next, I had to find hope. I found that hope in a relationship with a Higher Power. Finally, I needed to slowly acknowledge and test the power I do have. I do this through recognizing my accomplishments and setting goals to grow me in a new direction. As I continue to do these things, I continue to grow and am able to rebuild my dignity and personhood. This enables me to redefine my femininity and to access the power I have within my soul.

Meditation for the day

I will focus on the God-given power that is mine to nourish and grow. I will seek wisdom from those I trust and recognize the gifts I have to share with others.

Prayer for the day

I pray to be of service to other women that need support. I pray to be strong enough to be humble and kind enough to be generous with the gifts I have been given.

Mantra for the day

      I am of service to others and give back what has been given to me. I am of service to others and give back what has been given to me. I am of service to others.

Reflection for the day

_____

_____

_____

_____

_____

_____

_____

_____

_____

_____

_____

_____

_____

_____

_____

Thought for the day

It has been said that we all need to find our own smile. Sometimes this is easy to do and sometimes it requires a great deal of effort. What most of us can agree upon is this; other people do indeed influence us. Sometimes their impact can be beneficial, other times it is distracting. We all need people to one degree or another, but we mustn't allow them to dissuade our spiritual growth. I need always to remember that my smile and my happiness are my responsibility. When I earnestly turn to my God and do as I think would be pleasing, I find a foundation for happiness that no one or any event can challenge. I need to free myself from the notion that people can make me happy. My spiritual life and my new set of beliefs form the foundation of what I call happiness. When I feel myself rising to my spiritual potential I can feel my true calling as an enlightened woman and I am fulfilled.

Meditation for the day

Today I will meditate and try to differentiate between the joy of human happiness and Divine happiness. I look back and see how well-meaning people have countless times challenged my ability to maintain a harmonious spirit. I then look to my spiritual life for its consistency and permanence in my life. I ask myself from where my lasting happiness will come.

Prayer for the day

I pray to be vigilant in my spiritual life. I pray to be ever mindful of the source of my true and everlasting joy. I pray to realize that my smile does indeed come from the love placed in me by my God.

Mantra for the day

 I have found my smile, it is mine to keep. I have found my smile, it is mine to keep. I have found my smile, it is mine to keep.

Reflection for the day

_____

_____

_____

_____

_____

_____

_____

_____

_____

_____

_____

_____

_____

_____

_____

Thought for the day

Gift: anything given, a present; a special talent or aptitude. Yep, that's me! A great definition of me! As a queen and a goddess I need to recognize my talents and aptitudes. I also need to see that these qualities were both God-given and personally developed. My faith in my Spirit and myself continues to grow. This is true of my willingness to take on new thought and cast off old, unbeneficial beliefs. My life is also a gift, and I will treat it like any other gift that I would receive. Just think of the spiritual heartache if I did not treat myself as the treasure God intended me to be. Whenever a gift is not joyously received, it has fallen into the hands of the ignorant. No act of kindness or generosity should fail to be received in a like manner. Today I receive my personality and my life with a thankful heart.

Meditation for the day

Today I contemplate how best to share the gift that I am with others. I want them to feel the compassion, the full heart, the warmth of my spirit; thus I will share the gift. My time and energies are gifts as well. I want them to be well received; therefore I carefully choose with whom I share myself. For when I share me, I share my God. I am the gift, and I do not squander my talents on ignorant or mean-spirited people.

Prayer for the day

I pray to rightly use my talents for the benefit of all. I need to also remember that I am part of the whole. A goddess takes care of herself. I will be pampered, loved and esteemed. I treat myself as I would any other wonderful gift.

Mantra for the day
 I am the gift. I am the gift. I am the gift.

Reflection for the day

_____

_____

_____

_____

_____

_____

_____

_____

_____

_____

_____

_____

_____

_____

_____

_____

_____

Thought for the day

When I wander and wonder the most, I am separated from my spiritual connection. When I abandon my spiritual listening post, I open myself more to the harsh criticisms of man. Without my spiritual anchor I have no choice but to let myself and others judge me. Experience dictates that these earthly judgments are far harsher than the Divine ones. If I choose not to allow a kind, loving Spirit into my life in order to guide me, I am stuck with my own best thinking! Unless I can be reasonably certain that I have been purged of selfishness and dishonest thinking, it would be in my best interest to strive to maintain my spiritual growth above all. From my God comes my strength, wisdom, and passion. These are the spiritual benefits that enable me to lead effectively. Unless I can abandon myself completely, I would be presumptuous to believe that anyone else could place themselves under my care and guidance.

Meditation for the day

Surrender to win. This simple concept can take a lifetime to employ. I also realize that if I can meet the demands of my need to surrender, then so can the people in my life. Just as I find release in surrender, so they will as well. As a Spirit-filled woman I will give and receive surrender in my life. This free flow of positive energy will invigorate all and cast our net of freedom from selfishness and dishonest thinking.

Prayer for the day

I pray to graciously surrender to my God. I pray to keep the positive flow of love alive by this give-and-take of the surrender of self. When I abandon self, only then am I free to receive my spiritual nourishment from which flows all goodness and grace.

Mantra for the day
      I surrender to win. I surrender to win. I surrender to win.

Reflection for the day

_____

_____

_____

_____

_____

_____

_____

_____

_____

_____

_____

_____

_____

_____

_____

_____

Thought for the day

Spiritual warfare or spiritual welfare, the option is mine. I have a choice today in how I feel about and address my spiritual needs. In the past I was coerced into acknowledging a set of beliefs that I wasn't always comfortable with. I was often made to feel at odds, like the Forces were my foe. This type of spiritual division cost me much wasted time and energy. I had all of the 'how could' and 'what will' questions, coupled with several drastically different outcomes. Some of these possible outcomes sounded much better than the others, but there was no definitive answer with which I could satisfy myself. One day I heard a man speak and he helped me more than any other to understand. He simply said; "If God is all powerful and God is all knowing, it only makes sense, that if God was going to get me he would have had me by now!" Whoa, that settles it. God is NOT out to get me; the war is over, let the welfare begin! Spiritual welfare; a state of doing well. Today, united at last, We are doing quite well.

Meditation for the day

Perhaps the teachings weren't bad maybe just my understanding of them was flawed. I need to ask myself and those that I love and respect all of the spiritual questions that I have. There are good, knowledgeable people and there are wonderful writings on the understanding and works of the Great Spirit. I owe it to myself to satisfy my spiritual needs.

Prayer for the day

I pray for the ability to identify the spiritual questions that I have. I ask for the willingness and humility to find the people and the resources that will enable me to quench my spiritual thirst.

Mantra for the day
  I will satisfy my spiritual thirst. I will satisfy my spiritual thirst. I will satisfy my spiritual thirst.

Reflection for the day

_____

_____

_____

_____

_____

_____

_____

_____

_____

_____

_____

_____

_____

_____

_____

_____

Thought for the day

The dating experience can be difficult. Many men pursue their intended with the best of intentions. They are polite, respectful and yield to the wishes of the woman that they are interested in. Some of these men say things like "what show would you like to see" or "where would you like to go for dinner" or "whatever pleases you would be fine with me". It would seem that this whole process is centered on making the woman happy and following her in her role as leader. However, more times than not, once the courtship is over things take an ugly turn. Once he is confident that she is 'his'; then he sets out to make her 'his girlfriend' or 'his wife' At this point he begins to make decisions for them both and he assumes the leadership role with no intention of ever giving it back. Problems develop and the man can't understand what is 'wrong with her'. What is 'wrong with her' is that she has just been demoted with her consent from queen to a common possession.

Meditation for the day

I will look back and see how my disempowerment took place. With the best of intentions for a more meaningful life, I let my guard down and was taken advantage of. I will look at the folly of societal beliefs that continue to encourage women to follow this flawed thinking and to devalue themselves in the name of 'love'.

Prayer for the day

I pray to rightly see the flaws in the ways of 'love'. I pray to stay strong and to provide for my own security. I ask God to remind me that real love benefits me and never demeans me. I need to stay spiritually focused especially when romance is involved.

Mantra for the day
   I will not give up my queendom for a relationship. I will not give up my queendom for a relationship. I will not give up my queendom for a relationship.

Reflection for the day

_____

_____

_____

_____

_____

_____

_____

_____

_____

_____

_____

_____

_____

Thought for the day

When trouble strikes and we see a person in emotional distress, how often do we ask, 'are you going to be okay'? Inevitably they will respond,' yes I'll be fine'. Both these statements take us out of today. They also suggest that we are somehow flawed. Emotions are just emotions they do not signify our worthiness. We are just as fine as we need to be, today, tomorrow, and forevermore. This is the day that we are working on; today, just today. When I project my happiness, welfare, and emotional well-being into the future, I am unable to live fully today. I need always to remember that I do have the power, I do have the love of my God, and I am doing all I can right now to meet the current demands placed upon me. When I claim my place in the universe and live well today, my future is bright and comes about naturally.

Meditation for the day

I concentrate on this day. This is the day that my God has given me and WE are doing fine! I do not let myself or others trade my life today for the future. I do not put off the work I need to do today in favor of a dream to come. I have this day and I live it to the best of my ability.

Prayer for the day

I ask to stay centered on this day. I ask that I can search both within and without to find the power and grace to live this life one day at a time, with hope, faith and gratitude.

Mantra for the day

Just for today, I am useful and fulfilled. Just for today, I am useful and fulfilled. Just for today, I am useful and fulfilled.

Reflection for the day

_____

_____

_____

_____

_____

_____

_____

_____

_____

_____

_____

_____

_____

_____

_____

_____

_____

Thought for the day

Listening is a word that is often used but many times discounted in favor of willful justification. Listening is a part of the vicarious learning process. As I learn by watching and listening, I don't need to reinvent the wheel each time I reach a state of indecision. It is important to learn to listen effectively to improve my station in life. Information is power. I want to enhance my personal power by using this as an effective means of leadership in my life. I need to listen to the subtle cues of others to learn of their needs. This allows me to assist them in finding their joy. Men are drawn to dominant, forceful women. As I listen, I am able to discern those I am able to best teach to meet my needs. This not only pleases me, but it brings the men much comfort and joy in their service to women.

Meditation for the day

Today I listen carefully to what the people in my life are saying. Do the people I work with defer to my judgment? Do men ask and try to find ways to be pleasing to me? Can I see the willingness of certain men and reaffirm the knowledge of my superiority through their actions? Isn't it time that I realize the truth and rise to my true station as a goddess?

Prayer for the day

Today I pray for awareness to actively listen and internalize what I hear. I desire to open my heart and mind to the possibilities of increasing my power and leadership skills. I ask to listen to that voice that cries from within to claim my freedom and power as a queen.

Mantra for the day

Listening enhances my life and my freedom.
Listening enhances my life and my freedom.
Listening enhances my life and my freedom.

Reflection for the day

_____

_____

_____

_____

_____

_____

_____

_____

_____

_____

_____

_____

_____

_____

_____

_____

_____

_____

Thought for the day

I once had a friend ask me this simple question. He said, "What is between the colors of black and white?" I knew that this was a trick question so I took my time, gathered my thoughts and responded, "gray". Well, he smiled and said "nope, it's all the colors of the rainbow". Once again I was innocently called upon to review my self-imposed limitations. I want to live in the rainbow. I want to experience all the flavors of life without those self-imposed restrictions and negative thoughts. If life were flavors of ice cream it would not be chocolate or vanilla, it would be Neapolitan! As children this little three flavor multicolored delight was at every party because it provided something for everyone. Well, that's what this life is supposed to be. It is supposed to provide joy and meet the needs of everyone. How many opportunities have I missed living in a small, gray world? I will expand my view from here all the way through the rainbow. I choose to live in color and flavor with the satisfaction that I am entitled to all the joy this world has to offer.

Meditation for the day

I once again view the folly of my former thinking. My previous views were not necessarily wrong; they were just constraining and narrow. I want to live without restraint. I want to be free to find and live in the rainbow of life. Color, flavor, new belief; MMMMMMMM it's good to be queen.

Prayer for the day

I pray to seek opportunities, new ideas and growth. I ask to be forever mindful of the simple saying; nothing changes if nothing changes. I ask that all of God's children can eternally enjoy rainbows and Neapolitan flavors free of their self-imposed, apathetic, gray existence.

Mantra for the day
I live in the rainbow of life. I live in the rainbow of life. I live in the rainbow of life.

Reflection for the day

_____

_____

_____

_____

_____

_____

_____

_____

_____

_____

_____

_____

_____

_____

_____

Thought for the day

It has been said that what we resist persists. What causes me to resist my personal evolution? I really can't think of anyone more deserving of a good life than me! So what holds me to the past? Part of my resistance to growth is all of the negative ideas, comments and limitations I heard while growing up. That was then, this is now. I am no longer defined by others. I have the liberty to set myself free from my own resistance to change. If my goal is to change, evolve, find my power and become an active, useful member of society I need to cast off the fetters of the past. Today I am open to new thought. I am not constrained by my fear of failure. Today I can see what I used to call failure is indeed my friend, not my enemy. My fear of failure has often created my resistance. New thought, new belief and a fearless, fail-proof future will defeat the resistance that has impeded my growth.

Meditation for the day

Today I meditate on this simple truth. Failure is not failure, it is motivation. If I am to create a new and a brighter future for myself and those I love, it will be by using all of my resources. I seek to learn fully from the past so that I do not repeat it.

Prayer for the day

I pray to rightly see what I perceived as failure for what it is; motivation to grow and change. I pray to fully realize that today's faith will outlive yesterday's fear. I ask for the power to turn the past to good account and allow me to better serve my God and the people in my life.

Mantra for the day

I have no fear of failure for it does not exist. I have no fear of failure for it does not exist. I have no fear of failure for it does not exist.

Reflection for the day

_____

_____

_____

_____

_____

_____

_____

_____

_____

_____

_____

_____

_____

_____

_____

_____

_____

Thought for the day

I am free to believe anything I want to believe. I have my own sense of worth and consciousness which provides my boundaries. I'm tired of trying to meet someone else's expectations and be subject to their limitations. I decide who I am and what I do. I surround myself with like-minded people who support the new life that I have created. I no longer seek people to justify my actions. Today I seek out open-minded people that share my joy. I have changed! I am a queen and I do not apologize for my freedom, my power, or my joy! Enlightened women support me, and enlightened men succumb to my beauty and innate strength. I see no reason to feel the guilt that society imposes on intelligent, strong-minded, loving women.

Meditation for the day

I can measure my growth by my past, but I will not revisit the past with a wondering heart. I am where I have chosen to be. The past did not meet my needs, so I left it behind for a brighter and more fulfilling future.

Prayer for the day

I pray to my loving and understanding God to set me free from my past. This enables me to find the release that I need to be the woman that I am placed here to be. I pray to be encouraging to the children of my Creator. I ask for the humility not to demean the irrelevant males that still clamor for my attention.

Mantra for the day

I believe differently, I have changed. I believe differently, I have changed. I believe differently, I have changed.

Reflection for the day

_____

_____

_____

_____

_____

_____

_____

_____

_____

_____

_____

_____

_____

_____

_____

_____

Thought for the day

A man is most vulnerable while in bed. It is here that he can be made whole or crushed by our words or responses. His ego is open to our approval. He gives me the power to make him or break him contingent upon my appraisal of his efforts. This is why a wise woman will take the lead in these matters. If he needs to succeed (and he does), then it is up to me to set the agenda and the standard so he can be fulfilled. It is an act of kindness to supply the parameters of success. Most intelligent men seek to please in the bedroom. It is up to me to take that willingness to please and the need for ego satisfaction into our day-to-day lives. As he learns that my satisfaction is paramount, he becomes much more willing to work for my approval in all areas of life. A wise man will seek to ever improve his service to his queen for it is only in HER approval that he can satisfy what his ego calls manhood.

Meditation for the day

I look to see how his ego need to succeed can enhance my life. If he is willing to seek my approval in the bedroom, it is up to me to ensure that he seeks my approval in the living room and all throughout life. I meditate on how best to have my needs as a goddess met while enabling him to find his own fulfillment through my satisfaction.

Prayer for the day

I seek through prayer to find a means of personal fulfillment for all. I pray to better understand his need to satisfy me, and I look for opportunities to create success for him through my personal satisfaction and happiness.

Mantra for the day

My satisfaction is pleasing for all. My satisfaction is pleasing for all. My satisfaction is pleasing for all.

Reflection for the day

_____

_____

_____

_____

_____

_____

_____

_____

_____

_____

_____

_____

_____

_____

_____

_____

_____

Thought for the day

Ahh, new love! There is nothing quite like the exhilarating ride that new romance provides. New love is wonderful. It is full of hope and wonder. However, once the newness fades, I become curious as to why I didn't see the flaws in my prospective lover until it was too late. They say love is blind and there is an element of truth in this statement. Worse yet, is that new love is often deaf too. How does he talk about his former relationships? Does he speak of his mother with the reverence that she deserves? Does he interrupt and seem more concerned with himself than me? Are his interests and bonds mostly with male friends and sports, or is he interested in humanitarian efforts? We need to employ our intellectual faculties BEFORE we involve our heart and bodies. This is an excellent area to maintain cognitive discipline of myself. If he cannot or will not respect my beliefs and intellectual capabilities, need we go any further?

Meditation for the day

Is it possible for me to learn from my mistakes? Can I really expect to find a better life if I make the effort? The answer is yes indeed. There are many examples of my growth to call upon that validates my progress. However, I must always remember that 'nothing changes if nothing changes'. Because I want a new and better life, I need to apply new and better life skills.

Prayer for the day

I need to always remember that my life is worth working for. I ask for wisdom and strength to see my former faults and make the changes that I truly desire. I pray for clarity of mind before I open my heart and body.

Mantra for the day

   In romance, my mind will rule my heart. In romance, my mind will rule my heart. In romance my mind will rule my heart.

Reflection for the day

_____

_____

_____

_____

_____

_____

_____

_____

_____

_____

_____

_____

_____

_____

_____

_____

Thought for the day

My mind must remain open if I am to change. As I look back at all of the old beliefs and traditions I failed to challenge, I can see how and why I stayed emotionally stuck. We are taught to go with the flow, honor tradition and not to make waves. This is a perfect recipe for a stagnant life. I want a life worth living, a life of passion as defined by me not the voices of the past. It is important to find the courage to challenge and change the traditions in my own family that I find distasteful. Tradition is our tie to the past. I have no desire to drag the misfortunes of my painful past into the future. I am open-minded and free to decide who and what I honor today and in the future.

Meditation for the day

It is my life and I am free to create new memories and traditions for my friends, my family and myself. I need to remember that as a grown, independent woman I am free to decide what my future will be and who will be there.

Prayer for the day

I pray for the enlightenment and power to write my own life script. The future is mine to claim, not theirs to guide. I pray for discernment in my choices and values concerning my future and the lives of those whom I love.

Mantra for the day

A new life requires new choices. A new life requires new choices. A new life requires new choices.

Reflection for the day

_____

_____

_____

_____

_____

_____

_____

_____

_____

_____

_____

_____

_____

_____

_____

_____

Thought for the day

      We are all faced with trials in life. Many losses punctuate our experiences: death, divorce, loss of relationships, children growing and leaving home, etc. Nietzsche said that what doesn't kill use makes us stronger. That almost sounds cruel to someone going through a loss, but it's oh so true. Each time we experience the trials of life, be they a devastating loss or a daily trial of a single mother trying to balance her budget so her daughter can continue dance, we grow in our abilities. Our ability to think, reason, manage, grieve, help others is strengthened. Our desire for further growth is thus fueled. As we grow and say to ourselves that 'I made it through this', we find a confidence that allows us to take on larger challenges and continue our growth. As difficult as it may seem, we welcome trials as they do make us strong. Ask yourself, "What did I learn from this? How can I grow?"

Meditation for the day

      My thoughts turn to my experiences and what I have learned. My focus is on the lessons and strength I have gained from the trials. I recognize the hurt and embrace the growth the trial brings.

Prayer for the day

      God, give me strength to work through trials with my head held high, knowing that I am learning something very powerful. I ask for continued blessings and grace to deal with the difficult and learn the lesson.

Mantra for the day

I am learning my lessons with gratitude. I am learning my lessons with gratitude.

Reflection for the day

_____

_____

_____

_____

_____

_____

_____

_____

_____

_____

_____

_____

_____

_____

_____

_____

_____

_____

Thought for the day

I am wary of attacks. They distress me because if I am not spiritually fit, I often defend myself. A defense is an attack. Once this process of attack and defend is underway, chance of successful resolution is minimal. Once an argument begins, usually both parties switch from trying to find a solution to trying to prove that they are right. This is a sad and sick, ego-feeding game in which I no longer choose to participate. When I am fit spiritually there is nothing to prove. I'm just okay and there is not a soul on this earth that can change my level of emotional comfort without my consent. This shows once again that my spiritual welfare must come before everything for it is my belief and faith that give me the strength to honor myself.

Meditation for the day

I honor myself and my spiritual beliefs when I can remain calm and thoughtful during difficult situations. I need to look back at some of the unfortunate incidents of my past to remind me that no one ever wins an argument. Right, wrong, or indifferent; when I give up my peace of mind, I suffer. I no longer have a desire to suffer.

Prayer for the day

I pray to remember that I am always safe and protected. There is no need to defend myself. I ask that I not lower myself to the point of conflict with others. I will always remember that I have chosen to live in love, not turmoil.

Mantra for the day

My peace is a reflection of my faith. My peace is a reflection of my faith. My peace is a reflection of my faith.

Reflection for the day

_____

_____

_____

_____

_____

_____

_____

_____

_____

_____

_____

_____

_____

_____

_____

Thought for the day

I am so very strong and versatile.
Sometimes it's fun to count all of the people that I
do or have loved. I can love like a daughter, a
sister, a mom, a friend and a queen. I have so very
much love in me to share that I am sometimes
amazed. In all areas I need to concentrate my
efforts on my outpouring of love and not on the love
that I receive. My God placed me here to be a
distributor of Divine love. As I realize that my love
comes from my Creator I am no longer be
concerned with the earthly reception of it. What
truly matters is how and whom I love. My ability to
love pleases me and my Spirit greatly.

Meditation for the day

When I strip away all the ugliness of life, all
that is left is all that matters; LOVE. I realize that
there are many distractions to keep me from my
primary purpose, but I do not waver in my efforts to
be the best lover that I can be. I meditate on this
simple truth. When it comes to love, one cannot
give it away quicker than God gives it back.

Prayer for the day

I pray to remember my primary purpose on
this earth and beyond. I pray not to give in to the
petty distractions of life. I ask for the strength to
continue to improve my ability and willingness to
love.

Mantra for the day

I am a good lover. I am a good lover. I am
a good lover.

Reflection for the day

_____

_____

_____

_____

_____

_____

_____

_____

_____

_____

_____

_____

_____

_____

_____

_____

Thought for the day

Women in the workplace are often at a distinct disadvantage. Many men continue to see women in a subservient role, as the weaker sex, unable to make strong decisions and stick by them. It's sad, no tragic, that because of family, society, and self-conditioning, many women assume that role, some willing, some begrudgingly. We can change this by beginning to believe the truth. Many women are as intelligent, or more so than most men. Women have an increased perspective to see the bigger picture due to the fact that they have greater access to their emotional and intellectual presence. Most women have a stronger developed sense of compassion. With this sense, they are able to express their superiority without the constraints that can be placed on them by a patriarchal society. We are not subservient or weak. Take the lead, give direction and provide the wisdom that only you as a woman possess.

Meditation for the day

Today my focus is on my unique gifts as a woman. I cherish these gifts and work to continue growing. I have the leadership qualities and the compassionate wisdom that is original to my gender. I refuse to be made to believe I am less than in the workplace because of my female identity. I have the competence, intelligence and emotional strength to face any situation as well as the wisdom and guidance to put those gifts into force.

Prayer for the day

I ask for courage to face the male domination in the workplace and life in general. I pray for humility in expressing the gifts I have.

May I always be respectful while being bold in my assertions that I am a capable and strong woman.

Mantra for the day
 I have the strength and capabilities to flourish in any work environment. I have the strength and capabilities to flourish in any work environment.

Reflection for the day

_____

_____

_____

_____

_____

_____

_____

_____

_____

_____

_____

_____

_____

_____

Thought for the day

Life can be painful and the people in it can be hurtful and disappointing. This is all the more reason that I need to claim my power as queen. So many times in the past I have been drawn into painful events through no fault of my own. My ideals have been trampled on and my heart has been broken. My experiences have shown me the best and the worst of love and life. I've been bruised but never broken. What have I learned? I've learned and come to believe that if I have to cry myself to sleep, it will be because of my mistakes NOT someone else's! I am a big girl and I can stand or fall based on my own choices. In this regard I must realize that there are no failures, only opportunities to learn.

Meditation for the day

My tears don't taste as bad if they are of my own creation. In the past my tears have been influenced by others and coupled with their shame, fear and doubt. I have erroneously taken on others' shortcomings as my own and cried myself to sleep as if their pain and burdens were mine to claim. I shall not taint my tears with the mistakes and vindictiveness of others.

Prayer for the day

I pray for the strength to endure the pain I may have created. I ask to learn the lessons offered. I also seek to resist the evil of others so that my life will not be stifled with their burdens.

Mantra for the day

A queen claims her own tears. A queen claims her own tears. A queen claims her own tears.

Reflection for the day

_____

_____

_____

_____

_____

_____

_____

_____

_____

_____

_____

_____

_____

_____

_____

_____

_____

_____

_____

Thought for the day

There seems to be some kind of sinister plot against fun and joyfulness. We often hear 'it's time to grow up', or 'stop that laughing and clowning around'. Yes, it is time to grow up, and it is time to make, develop, and execute a workable plan for our lives. However, we need to remember that maturity need not be void of fun and laughter. Cheerfulness and laughter bring our true beauty to the surface. I want the world to know me by my heart as well as for my accomplishments. Balance is the key. There is a time for all the emotional seasons that we experience. Laughter makes for usefulness. We can't very well claim to be a representative of a loving, fulfilled God and then remain sullen and dejected. We were given the gift of laughter and joy to share so that we can be agents of delight in the lives of others.

Meditation for the day

I take a balanced view of my life. I see that there is a time for work, a time for sorrow and also a time for unrestrained joy and laughter. I wasn't placed in this life to be miserable. I have the power of God, people and my own abilities to create and maintain any level of joyousness I wish to claim.

Prayer for the day

I pray to live the joy of my God. I ask to be given the ability to love and inspire the joyful hearts of others. I want my Creator's world to be a happy place. I am willing to do my part to create and carry joy to all who would receive it.

Mantra for the day

I will develop and share my joy. I will develop and share my joy. I will develop and share my joy.

Reflection for the day

_____

_____

_____

_____

_____

_____

_____

_____

_____

_____

_____

_____

_____

_____

_____

_____

_____

Thought for the day

Disappointment and heartache; it seems these two come around on a regular basis. I was counseling a woman in prison one day. She was crying hard and trying to get me to understand that being there made her feel 'like I'm dying'. I asked her 'do you really feel like you are dying?' Her reply was a very emotional and tearful 'yes'. I then told her to go ahead and die, because we all need to die to be reborn. I have fought change and emotional death for years and all I have done is prolong the pain before my rebirth. Just suppose that I could let go with the knowledge that renewal is mine to claim. If I could move on gracefully I would save much time, heartache, and energy.

Meditation for the day

I reflect on my unwillingness to let go of the hurtful past. I can become a queen and a goddess whenever I am willing to let go of the misinformation I was given by the patriarchy. My mental, emotional, and spiritual rebirth is to be gleefully accepted not fearfully rejected. I no longer postpone my progress. I let go of the pain and embrace my future as the independent, joyous woman I am destined to be.

Prayer for the day

I ask that I move on toward my emotional death and rebirth with a quiet quickness that will define my new character. I pray to be allowed to demonstrate the power of faith in my life. I know others are watching, and God and I will move forward with assurance and grace.

Mantra for the day
    I am reborn. I am reborn. I am reborn.

Reflection for the day

_____

_____

_____

_____

_____

_____

_____

_____

_____

_____

_____

_____

_____

_____

_____

_____

_____

Thought for the day

I will not devalue myself by adopting the present day standards of the patriarchy. As a woman I have a worldwide sisterhood that is ready to work for change. A world based on love, not fear, is our goal. Men are the traditional warriors and the world we currently live in defines their best efforts. We find ourselves in a world of plenty where most people live without; a world of fear when most want to love. This world is divided and conquered for the benefit of the greedy few. When women step up and overthrow these flawed political beliefs, love will reign supreme. Women are not warriors, for we know the fallacy of war. Women do not withhold, for we know the gift of love. Women do not divide, for there is power and love in unity.

Meditation for the day

Today I consider my level of involvement with the flawed patriarchy. I ponder on my level of compliance to a failed system. Now and in the future, I will talk of change and challenge beliefs to work for a better world, a world fit for our most precious gifts; our children!

Prayer for the day

I pray for the boldness to challenge the sinful world that man has created. I will build my relationships with other like-minded women and continue our faithful assent to true power and a more peaceful loving world.

Mantra for the day

The future is female. The future is female.
The future is female!

Reflection for the day

_____

_____

_____

_____

_____

_____

_____

_____

_____

_____

_____

_____

_____

_____

_____

_____

_____

_____

Thought for the day
I was taught to be a 'nice' girl. Upon reflection I can truly say that either I missed their point entirely or I understood it all too well. With the changes that I am seeking for myself I see where my former understanding was terribly flawed. Apparently I was supposed to sacrifice my own well-being and happiness for the good of others (men). I was supposed to limit my sexuality to the standards of my narrow-minded community. I was to remain meek and compliant, never to complain or seek to promote my own well-being. Nice? Yes, indeed very nice for them! I'm 100% behind the concept of altruism and the elimination of the 'self' but not at the expense of my personal dignity or respect. When I start to compromise myself for the benefit of another, I am headed back to being that 'nice girl' I'm trying to leave behind. Today I consider 'nice' to be taking care of myself and those that I allow into my world.

Meditation for the day
The more things change, the more they stay the same. In my relationships I seek 'nice' men. I expect them to promote and secure for my welfare without diminishing their own personal dignity. In this way, they are allowed to learn a new kind of respect for themselves that comes with service to an enlightened woman. Today compliant men are drawn to my strength and recognize my character. My new and powerful nature draws service-minded men to me. I revel in the changes of perception that I have experienced. Today I, too, have expectations of 'nice' and the people who can meet my standards will be welcome to become a part of my life.

Prayer for the day

I ask for the ongoing ability to live in the truth. I did not then, and have no desire now, to fit into role of 'nice' that the world had planned for me. Today I see 'nice' as allowing a male to serve me, to meet my requirements that will ensure my satisfaction. I pray to be grateful for my choices and the ongoing ability to meet others' needs by allowing them to be who they really are.

Mantra for the day

Nice no longer means 'nice'. Nice no longer means 'nice'. Nice no longer means 'nice'.

Reflection for the day

_____

_____

_____

_____

_____

_____

_____

_____

_____

_____

_____

Thought for the day

When I set the boundaries for my life and the people in it, I must remember the purpose of boundaries. If the boundaries that I set are too strict I often feel uncomfortable and want to rebel against them. If these same parameters are too loose, I feel fear and uncertainty. The purpose of setting boundaries is so that I can remain comfortable and efficient without too many emotional distractions. When I share expectations and goals for others in my life, this allows them to excel. I do not abide with rebellion in the realm of my relationships. Therefore, I need to provide workable, comfortable parameters for those I love. A firm and steady set of guidelines provides the stability needed so that our interactions are constant, comfortable and without doubt or worry. The effort I make to build structure in my enlightened life is returned in kind.

Meditation for the day

I consider what makes a good leader. Just because I have elevated my position in life does not mean that I can neglect those yet to come. The sisters that seek my help and others that seek my guidance all need to know of my wants, desires, and boundaries. A queen is generous in the information of her expectations so that those who serve may readily succeed and be made whole.

Prayer for the day

I pray to be a good example for my sisters and a righteous leader of all. By living within my own guidelines for life, I draw people to me. In that way, I am able to share the goodness of a spiritually motivated lifestyle.

Mantra for the day

Good boundaries make for a good life. Good boundaries make for a good life. Good boundaries make for a good life.

Reflection for the day

_____

_____

_____

_____

_____

_____

_____

_____

_____

_____

_____

_____

_____

_____

_____

_____

_____

_____

_____

Thought for the day
 I once received a letter from a dear friend.
She said she feared her heart would harden due to
all of the pain acquired over the years. There are a
many reasons why people hurt us.
As I pondered these hurts, this simple phrase came
to me. "They didn't do it <u>to me</u>, they did it <u>for
themselves</u>". When we can internalize this concept
two things happen. One is that it takes the power
away from the offender, and the other is that it takes
me out of the victim role. They don't need any
more power, and while the victim role can be sadly
useful, it's not as much fun as the hero role. As I
rightly distance myself from the pain and injury of
the past, I am well on my way to being the
enlightened woman that I choose to be. I am my
own independent hero and I refuse to own their
sickness or their feelings!

Meditation for the day
 Today I dismantle the pain of the past. As I
relive each painful situation I can truly see that it
really wasn't personal until I personalized it. The
power was mine until I gave it away. If I take me
out of the situation and place anyone else there,
those same people who hurt me would also hurt the
others because they are acting on their own behalf.
The victim is not a victim just an unfortunate
participant in the sick games that sick people play.
It is not personal unless I allow it to be.

Prayer for the day
 It has been said that hurt people hurt people.
When I get honest and put my desires aside it is
much easier to see the liabilities that people bring
into my life. I pray to associate with a better group

of people. I will know them through improved communication skills, patience, and a sincere desire to know them by their deeds.

Mantra for the day

They didn't do it to me, they did it for themselves. They didn't do it to me, they did it for themselves. They didn't do it to me, they did it for themselves.

Reflection for the day

_____

_____

_____

_____

_____

_____

_____

_____

_____

_____

_____

_____

Thought for the day

As I look back over my life, it is easy to see how I came to find myself here. This old, this discouraged, and most importantly this willing to change. While in school, everyone seemed united in their efforts to teach me what to think. We covered HIStory and all other subjects from the male perspective. However, no one seemed the least bit interested in teaching me HOW to think. Today I can see how I was limited. I know that if you teach a person how to think they can come to their own conclusions about what to think all by themselves. Some people would refer to these individuals as 'free thinkers'. When you consider the patriarchy and their agenda, it is easy to see why my freedom was traded for my compliance. The days of female compliance are over. Today I claim the right to use my superior female mind to promote my and my sister's agenda for a better world.

Meditation for the day

I look back, not to be disappointed but to learn. One more time I was counting on 'them' to meet my needs for education and life preparedness. I will make an effort to educate myself in female studies and HERstory so I can affirm my beliefs in female superiority. The more I learn, the more my circle of enlightened female friends will grow. There are other superior women out there. It is in my best interest to seek a new education based on my needs and wants. I will use all of the resources available to me to gain the life that I choose to live.

Prayer for the day

I pray to find the time, energy and
willingness to continue MY education. I continue
to explore and question as a way to develop my
learning skills in how to think!

Mantra for the day

Education is how I change. Education is
how I change. Education is how I change.

Reflection for the day

_____

_____

_____

_____

_____

_____

_____

_____

_____

_____

_____

_____

_____

Thought for the day

Being in love is a wondrous, grand adventure. Many will strive their entire lives for the perfect love relationship with another. The problem is, however, finding that one special person to meet our perceived needs, the one that accepts us exactly as we are and we them. Due to our rush and ultimate fear of being alone, we often settle for less than we deserve. We can find ourselves in situations that are less than desired, even dangerous. We have worked for change in ourselves and hoped for change in the other person. However, it is most important to learn to love ourselves first. Spend time with you, get to know who you are, your likes and dislikes. Be comfortable in your own skin in all situations. Then you will refuse to settle. You will find an inner strength that will attract that one 'perfect' person.

Meditation for the day

I refuse to sell myself short. I will focus my energy on knowing myself first. I will examine my beliefs, fears, desires and needs before hoping to share those with another.

Prayer for the day

I ask for wisdom and courage to face myself as I am. I desire a strong, but humble heart that can discern love as it is meant for me. I pray to be able to share this with the person that will treat me as I deserve to be treated.

Mantra for the day

I am comfortable in my own skin. I allow
that comfort in me to guide my choices today. I am
comfortable in my own skin.

Reflection for the day

_____

_____

_____

_____

_____

_____

_____

_____

_____

_____

_____

_____

_____

_____

_____

Thought for the day

The power that a woman possesses needs to be used in a wise and loving way. To assert our power to cause pain or bitterness in others shows weakness and inner resentment for whom we are. Our place in life has not always given us the benefits or the accolades that are so deserved, however, that does not give us the right to be cruel and shameful in our actions. It is up to us to show the world a better way, a day at a time.

Meditation for the day

I keep my focus on the power of the love I possess. I use this power to uplift and change the world, one day, one person, one attitude at a time. My behavior models a strength that does not harbor bitterness for what "should have been" but will glory in the courage of what *is* and what will be.

Prayer for the day

I pray to let go of inner resentments and aggression, especially in the face of those with little understanding of the women's struggle. I ask to show a level of compassion toward my fellow human beings that allows true strength and courage in the face of life's adversities.

Mantra for the day

     I use the power of love for goodness and greater gain for all. I use the power of love for goodness and greater gain for all. I use the power of love for goodness and greater gain for all.

Reflection for the day

_____

_____

_____

_____

_____

_____

_____

_____

_____

_____

_____

_____

_____

_____

Thought for the day

For many, many years a woman's job was considered her husband and family. Please understand that is a unique position and one that is a distinguished calling, however, as we have evolved as women, the desire to grow beyond that has unfolded and we often seek fulfillment in other areas as well. We, as women, are wonderfully gifted at multi-tasking. Whether we learned this from the necessity of being a single mother or out of a greater desire to experience that which had been denied, is not relevant. The point is that we are expanding and evolving. We are to be proud of the responsibilities that we choose to take on today. For the greater purpose of love and growth, we need recognize that we are an integral and prominent component.

Meditation for the day

Look within yourself and decide the roles you desire. Open yourself to growth and change and be not afraid of the direction. My focus today is learning to appreciate what I have accomplished and eagerly embrace the direction I am heading.

Prayer for the day

Oh Great Protector, we ask for guidance and wisdom in the choices we make regarding family and work. We ask for strength in our endeavors and that our direction is one that is in line with Your plan for our lives.

Mantra for the day

I have the strength and wisdom to lead and direct my life in positive ways. I have the strength and wisdom to lead and direct my life in positive ways.

Reflection for the day

_____

_____

_____

_____

_____

_____

_____

_____

_____

_____

_____

_____

_____

_____

_____

Thought for the day

The best thing about the future is that it only comes one day at a time. We all know these simple truths, but it seems that both socially and personally we are drawn into an uncertain future over which we have no control. Yes indeed, we should make plans, yes we should pray with expectation, but we must concentrate our efforts on this day. If I make the effort to improve my life today, tomorrow will take care of itself. A plan for the future without the work of today is lost. How can I best utilize my talents and the people in my life to create a better future starting today?

Meditation for the day

As a queen and goddess it is my duty to demand the best from those that serve me. Those that yield to me must work this day so that I can have a brighter and more comfortable future. It is my strength and power that draw people to me. My power applied today empowers those in service to evermore seek to provide for me.

Prayer for the day

I pray to be ever mindful of from where I came, to where I'm going and who I am today. I pray to be continually motivated to seek my personal power and growth so that I may provide a brighter future for those fortunate enough to share in my life.

Mantra for the day

I use this day to work for a brighter future. I use this day to work for a brighter future. I use this day to work for a brighter future.

Reflection for the day

_____

_____

_____

_____

_____

_____

_____

_____

_____

_____

_____

_____

_____

_____

_____

_____

_____

Thought for the day

The Beatles were right; all you need is love. We've all heard it, we all believe it, yet we often fail to cultivate it. I love God. I love my life. I love my kids. I love my relationship. I love my job. I love what's for dinner. I love that spot. I loved those times. I love those people. I love my dog. I love my cat. I love. I love. I love. So you see, it is clear, there is NEVER a shortage of love, NEVER. Sometimes I fail to give love its due. Sometimes I resist its existence and excellence. Sometimes I don't acknowledge, feel or share, but love IS and always will be. This free flow of universal goodness is the fuel that drives the engine of life. Without the recognition, acceptance and promotion of love; the quality of life itself becomes questionable. I wonder where I go in those strange mental blank spots when I can doubt the Power of an entire cosmos. Only my selfishness can stop the Power of universal love. Rather self-defeating and egotistical, isn't it? I humble myself before the Power of Love.

Meditation for the day

I give up! I surrender! The universe has more power to love than I have to resist! My resistance to life and love must stop. If I am to bring joy to the forefront it is necessary to embrace the love that is and always has been available.

Prayer for the day

I pray for an open mind and a compassionate heart. I pray to receive the universal goodness of which I am entitled. I pray for the wisdom to distribute the gifts with which I have been blessed.

Mantra for the day

All you need is love. All you need is love.
All you need is love. (sing it☺)

Reflection for the day

_____

_____

_____

_____

_____

_____

_____

_____

_____

_____

_____

_____

_____

_____

_____

_____

_____

Thought for the day

Why buy the cow when you can get the milk for free? Why buy the pig when you can get the sausage for free? Sounds like equality doesn't it? I've seen far too many women adopt male thinking in an effort to become equal. Why in the world would I want to be equal to a man? I was born female, physically, intellectually, and emotionally superior and I intend to stay that way! It is my standards and character that set me apart. I will not compromise my morals and my values. Free? I don't want anything for free, and I certainly don't give anything for free. I've worked hard to arrive at this position in my life and I have no intention of compromising it by lowering my standards to that of man.

Meditation for the day

I consider and celebrate my separateness. I am grateful for and maintain my superiority. The notion of equality is just an attempt to forestall the inevitable rise to female rule. I am not be diverted by this call to equality. I have no desire to be equal. I am a queen and a goddess I will never be equal!

Prayer for the day

Today I thank my God for giving me the gift of superiority at birth. Like any other gift, I need to maintain it if I expect it to last. Today I thank my God for the blessing of being born female.

I have no desire to be equal. I have no desire to be equal. I have no desire to be equal.

Reflection for the day

_____

_____

_____

_____

_____

_____

_____

_____

_____

_____

_____

_____

_____

_____

_____

_____

_____

_____

Thought for the day

In the past we have sought out aggressive, arrogant men in our relationships simply because we were unable to acknowledge and rely on our own personal power. We grew up with visions of Hercules, Tarzan and the strong fighting soldier. We were told of men's dominance in upper body strength, courage, and mathematical abilities. Our roles as women were diminished, "I'm just a housewife, a stay-at-home mother, a teacher, a nurse." These traditional female roles were often mocked. "I am emotional and make irrational decisions as such. I have cramps and PMS. I am less than..." BULLSHIT! My roles, as I define them are imperative to the continuation of humankind. The importance of what we accomplish cannot be measured and MUST NOT BE diminished. I am in charge of the path my life will take. It is important I claim my feminine power.

Meditation for the day

I refuse to be diminished as a woman. I take charge of my paths and define them to meet my personal needs. I do not allow others to define my worth or diminish any of my efforts.

Prayer for the day

I pray for balance in my thoughts, emotions and actions. I pray to remain Your humble servant in what I do today. I ask for the strength to battle the injustices I see and learn to choose my battles wisely.

Mantra for the day

I am strong and will not allow myself or my paths to be diminished by others. I am strong and will not allow myself or my paths to be diminished by others.

Reflection for the day

_____

_____

_____

_____

_____

_____

_____

_____

_____

_____

_____

_____

_____

_____

_____

_____

Thought for the day

Be who you are. After all there is only one uniquely individual you. There is no one else in this world who thinks like you, talks like you and acts like you. It is said we all have a "twin" somewhere on this earth. We may find someone that is very, very similar, yet no one possesses the conscious thought that you do. Learn to cherish the quirks, the differences that make you uniquely you. In our efforts to fit in we often neglect our uniqueness. Do not fear the distinction that sets you apart. Examine not only what you have to offer the world in your gracious beauty, but all you have to present to yourself. Focus on those wonderful qualities that define you. Recognize all we are gifted with and are so willing to share.

Meditation for the day

My focus is learning to be who I am. I am learning what it is about me that I want to love and know better. I am willing to suspend judgment on all the things I often consider embarrassing, trivial or useless. Once I do that I can have a level of comfort not yet experienced and appreciate my uniqueness to the fullest.

Prayer for the day

I ask for fearless wisdom in examining the traits I have in order to be of greater service to other women. I pray that I learn to appreciate myself for who I am and develop a sense of strength in all combined qualities.

Mantra for the day

I am uniquely designed for the purpose put before me. I am uniquely designed for the purpose put before me.

Reflection for the day

_____

_____

_____

_____

_____

_____

_____

_____

_____

_____

_____

_____

_____

_____

_____

_____

_____

_____

Thought for the day

Our new life, our hopes and dreams can only be accomplished with an element of risk. We need to risk giving up or losing what we have in an effort to acquire something better. Just the fact that I'm willing to improve myself and my position should tell me everything that I need to know. What I am willing to risk losing is really of little value or I wouldn't be compelled to move on. I must realize that life is a series of steps based on hope, risk and faith. The way I use these three components will indeed determine the course of my existence. I need the hope to launch my risk, and then I need to have my risk backed by faith. Faith will ease the great unknown that is the foundation of risk. In the end we will never get more than we are willing to risk. If we risk nothing we'll get nothing. In this regard there is fairness and equity in the universe.

Meditation for the day

I review how hope, risk, and faith can change my life. If my faith is strong, the fear of risk will diminish greatly. We all need to risk in order to grow, and we all need to grow to live and enjoy life. When I see the Divine plan the fear of risk seems inconsequential. Fortified with the love and grace of God my fears fall from me.

Prayer for the day

I pray to be relieved of any fear or panic that may unjustly deter my willingness to risk. As a goddess, I recognize my faith and the faith of those around me. Good information, superior intellect and a great and abiding faith make me fearless in the face of risk.

Mantra for the day

My hope propels me, my faith sustains me. My hope propels me, my faith sustains me. My hope propels me, my faith sustains me.

Reflection for the day

_____

_____

_____

_____

_____

_____

_____

_____

_____

_____

_____

_____

_____

_____

_____

_____

_____

_____

_____

Thought for the day
Today I acknowledge the evil within. It
would appear that I, and most of the people that I
know, try in vain to prove that they are all goodness
and joy. Well, it's just not true! I have dark
thoughts, fearful emotions, and unwanted desires
that often frighten me. I know that if I speak of
these things I will be ridiculed. I need to face my
darkness and embrace its untapped potential for
energy; energy that I can transform into whatever I
want. I need not fear my darkness. I must in time,
and possibly with help, walk up to the darkness,
embrace it, make peace with it leading it to the light
of hope. Fearing my darkness is lending energy I
need elsewhere. Fearing my evil is to fear myself!
If I abide in fear I'll never live in faith. Today I am
whole and not afraid or ashamed of my darkness.

Meditation for the day
I review the potentiality of my own evil.
With all the other transformations that I've made,
this is simply one more positive change. My faith
shields me as I do the work to liberate the darkness
and transform its untapped energy in light. This
illuminates my life and the lives of others. Ugliness
feeds on darkness. The light of the Spirit
transforms and nourishes all with goodness and joy.
My liberation is at hand.

Prayer for the day
I pray to make peace with the darkness as it
undergoes the transformation to light. I do not need
to kill the beast; I only need to tame it. Once tamed,
the beast will serve me, and I no longer fear it.
Freedom is mine.

Mantra for the day

      I do not fear the beast for it is mine to tame.
I do not fear the beast for it is mine to tame. I do
not fear the beast for it is mine to tame.

Reflection for the day

_____

_____

_____

_____

_____

_____

_____

_____

_____

_____

_____

_____

_____

_____

_____

_____

_____

_____

Thought for the day

Eleanor Roosevelt said, "No one can make you feel inferior without your permission." In first reading this, I was confused; it didn't make sense to my closed mind. As I began to change my view of myself, I found courage to begin recognizing and using my power for good. I began to understand that I am in charge of how I view myself and if that view is not of my liking, it is up to me to change it. I do have that power. Really.

Meditation for the day

My focus for the day will be on my personal power and how to begin accepting that. I will look for what I am most proud of in my thoughts and actions and make a plan to change that of which I am not proud. I will delight myself in the good in me and my world.

Prayer for the day

I pray to be wise and courageous in my self-assessment. I ask for guidance in what I choose to keep and nourish and what I choose to let go of today. I pray to share these gifts with others so that I will be worthy of those gifts.

Mantra for the day

I am wise and courageous. I am wise and courageous. I am wise and courageous.

Reflection for the day

_____

_____

_____

_____

_____

_____

_____

_____

_____

_____

_____

_____

_____

_____

_____

_____

_____

Thought for the day

When women in the workplace attempt to set limits and assert themselves in a leadership role, they are perceived as man-haters, the bitch, dried-up old prunes with nothing better to do with their lives than control others. They are often seen as cynical, possibly spurned by men in relationships and therefore have a need to assert themselves as a means of compensation. The true facets of their capabilities and wisdom are ignored and sometimes even ridiculed. We need to address this attitude immediately. This needs to be done with conviction. After all, we possess strength and qualities such as innate compassion, wisdom and self-confidence that all righteous leaders possess. As we continue to go in a positive direction, we assert ourselves in a firm but humble manner. This provides evidence to all that we hold such unique gifts as women that make it impossible to reject or discount them based on ridiculous and sexist ideation.

Meditation for the day

I look within myself today and inventory my gifts. I assess what I wish to keep and discard that which is no longer useful. I meditate on what is positive about the qualities I possess as a female leader and team member within the workplace.

Prayer for the day

I pray for strength to see myself as I am, not as perceived by those that are threatened by my strength. I ask for direction, humility and continued wisdom to be able to lead in a manner that is, as always, a credit to women everywhere.

Mantra for the day

I embrace the leadership skills with which I am gifted. I embrace the leadership skills with which I am gifted.

Reflection for the day

_____

_____

_____

_____

_____

_____

_____

_____

_____

_____

_____

_____

_____

_____

_____

_____

_____

Thought for the day

Obsession: an idea that will not yield to reason. These deadly little demons come in all shapes and forms. Some of the more common areas of obsession are alcohol, drugs, food (too much or too little), money, and of course, relationships. Whatever the problem is, we will find that invariably we have given power to the substance or person with which we are obsessed. Whatever we lend energy to grows. If one lends their energies to a bad relationship, it will continue to grow worse. This will not change until they decide to give their resources to the solution and not the problem. All obsessions take us away from a meaningful relationship with our Higher self. Our obsessions move us into a world of woeful emotions. This takes us away from the truth that with our intellect and spiritual guidance we can overcome any problem. I'm going to use my energy to improve my spiritual condition and to further my relationship with reality.

Meditation for the day

I see how obsessions have always diverted me from my primary purpose of elevating myself through the use of an enhanced spiritual life. When I become obsessed I have traded my relationship with God for an object or a person. This is not a very good trade as it always devalues me.

Prayer for the day

I pray to rightly see reality. I pray to yield to the forces of reason and not fall prey to the falsehoods of this life. I need to internalize the idea that love is not obsession. Reality and love should

be best friends not opponents in our heart and mind.
I pray to stay united with the truth.

Mantra for the day
      I will yield to reason. I will yield to reason.
I will yield to reason.

Reflection for the day

_____

_____

_____

_____

_____

_____

_____

_____

_____

_____

_____

_____

_____

_____

_____

Thought for the day

The people who turn to me for guidance are seeking guidance not control. They do not fear me they have faith in me. Therefore, I can best live and demonstrate that faith by being a benevolent woman. As I grow in faith and personal power people will be drawn to me. I do not need to fear their approach. They have come to me, be it for service or consult, because they have faith in my capabilities. While it is true that my new faith, power, and station in life are realities, sometimes, I feel like the last to acknowledge my growth. Perhaps, this is because I always used to put others first and did not accept my own worth. Today I need to have faith in the people that have faith in me. They are in my life and I value their opinion; they are kindhearted and trustworthy. I receive their opinions and faith in me with heartfelt gratitude for the changes that I have made and the woman that I have become.

Meditation for the day

I realistically look back and see the growth that I have made. Gone is the fear and uncertainty, gone is the need to be all things to all people, gone is the need to be validated through materialism or physical appearance. Today I view myself as a goddess and act accordingly. I shed the negativity of the past and have been given, though faith and grace, the power to guide and help others.

Prayer for the day

I pray for continued personal growth. I pray for discernment and the willingness to continue my work. I pray to realize that by holding myself to a

Higher standard, I am able to lead others to a greater cause as well.

Mantra for the day
I have changed. I have changed. I have changed.

Reflection for the day

_____

_____

_____

_____

_____

_____

_____

_____

_____

_____

_____

_____

_____

_____

_____

Thought for the day

We all have a past. Some of it is thrilling; some difficult to think about. We have made decisions that have led us in directions we never planned or imagined. All of those decisions were not the healthiest, however, we can use all we have experienced to assist our growth into a better person. It is important to look into the past long enough to see how it affects us now, but we don't want to live there. Learn the lessons you need from the experiences you've had and put the rest where it belongs…in the past.

Meditation for the day

I focus on what it is I need to learn from my past experiences. I let go of lingering shame or doubt over decisions I have made when circumstances did not materialize as I hope they would. Today, I look to this day with its blessings and seize the opportunity to learn.

Prayer for the day

I ask for discernment. I desire wisdom to know what to use and what to let go of. I pray I use my lessons from the past wisely and learn to make healthier choices based on what I have learned.

Mantra for the day

I am not negatively influenced by feelings about my past. I cherish this day. I am not negatively influenced by feelings about my past. I cherish this day.

Reflection for the day

_____

_____

_____

_____

_____

_____

_____

_____

_____

_____

_____

_____

_____

_____

_____

Thought for the day

When I am writing, I so enjoy listening to classical music. Now, I am a rocker at heart. Any day of the week, give me the Beatles, the Stones, Aerosmith, or Lynyrd Skynyrd. However, when I write, the strings, the piano, they soothe my soul. This is something I did not know until I tried it. What soothes your soul? What speaks to your heart? Is it nature? Music? What about meditation or spiritual journeys? The aroma of a rose can arouse in me such a sense of awe for nature's goodness. The blends of oils in a painting can speak to my heart. Reading prose or poetry provides me with a sense of peace. A quiet walk in the woods while listening to the birds gives me a sense of calm. Find what soothes you and present yourself with that gift on a regular basis. Try something new and expand your senses. After all, I am the gift, the goddess and I deserve to have time of my own to nurture those things in me that often get lost in the busyness of the day.

Meditation for the day

I will list the joys I now experience regarding the renewing of my spirit and soothing of my soul. I ponder what it is I would like to try and present that gift to myself. I will gift myself regularly to refresh the creativity and goodness that is given me.

Prayer for the day

My Creator, thank you for the gifts given. I praise the Maker of the universe and the awesome wonders that are contained therein. I ask for a presence and an infilling of the grandeur that is available to all.

Mantra for the day

I am blessed with the soothing wonder of our world. I am blessed with the soothing wonder of our world. I am blessed with the soothing wonder of our world.

Reflection for the day

_____

_____

_____

_____

_____

_____

_____

_____

_____

_____

_____

_____

_____

_____

_____

Thought for the day

A strong reputation is a reflection of character. Abraham Lincoln likens character to a tree and reputation its shadow. Unless the character of a person is solid, the reputation is flimsy and inaccurate. The unique thing about a shadow is that they can change shape depending on the light that is cast upon them. A very small thing can cast a large shadow or vice versa. However, the shadow can change but the character does not. Does your shadow, your reputation accurately reflect the depth of your character?

Meditation for the day

I think of the attributes I possess that are a measure of my character today. I strive to have the shadow be as solid as my character. I focus on ways I can strengthen each to be a strong example to others.

Prayer for the day

I ask for gentle guidance this day. I request a humble heart with strength that reflects love. I ask for assistance in building my character today and pray that the shadow be an honor to you God.

Mantra for the day

My character is like a strong, healthy tree. My character is like a strong, healthy tree. My character is like a strong, healthy tree.

Reflection for the day

_____

_____

_____

_____

_____

_____

_____

_____

_____

_____

_____

_____

_____

_____

_____

_____

_____

_____

Thought for the day

There are days when I feel lost, scattered. My mind just does not want to work the way I think it should. It's as if I have too many things floating around and I can't decide where to start. Try as I might, it becomes very difficult to get focused and accomplish the goals I have set for the day. When this happens I feel frustrated, I doubt my abilities and question my motives. It is days like these where I need to put one foot in front of another and just do it. I need to do what I have to do as if on auto-pilot; turn off my brain for a while and go. Small routines help: take a shower, make some breakfast, go for a walk. Lists are very good at times like these. The important thing here is to let go of inauthentic feelings of doubt and inadequacy. The powers of positive affirmations are great during these times. 'I am a strong and assertive woman.' 'I am a loving, caring woman with much to offer.' Do not let go of that which you know to be true about yourself due to short spans of confusion. Hang on to what you know.

Meditation for the day

Today I look to the strength I posses and let go of doubt and confusion. I know the core of who I am and refuse to be led astray by a day wherein I lack focus.

Prayer for the day

I pray for calmness of mind and convergence of thinking today. I ask to be reminded of what I have not what I lack.   O Great Spirit, provide me with focus and peace today. Help me to remember my purpose and not be derailed.

Mantra for the day

Put one foot in front of another and go. Put one foot in front of another and go. Put one foot in front of another and go.

Reflection for the day

_____

_____

_____

_____

_____

_____

_____

_____

_____

_____

_____

_____

_____

_____

_____

_____

_____

_____

Thought for the day

There are many ways to define my new mindset as queen and goddess. Some may think I am dominant, others would call me assertive and the uninformed may be brazen enough to refer to my behaviors as being a bitch. Today I define myself. I know my heart. By adopting a lifestyle of female rule, I am working to dismantle the selfish, hurtful, greed-filled life created by our male predecessors. My change of heart is first expressed at home and then with my friends. As my self-confidence grows, other women will join and move the world to a position of greater understanding. We need to remove ourselves, our children and our world from the hate and greed that currently propel it toward self-destruction.

Meditation for the day

The self-interest of man has taken society and the world to the edge. Women are seen to be feeding the poor and working for peace while men are seen to be promoting self-interest and violence. It will take a woman's heart, mind, and soul to replace the current self-interest and hate with love, warmth and tolerance. By taking control of and changing my life today, I am paving the way for the world change that is so desperately needed.

Prayer for the day

I pray to be given a greater vision of the world today. I pray to see that, yes indeed, I *can* change the world. My God changes the world one heart at a time. I ask to be given the willingness to accept the strength that I need to fortify my heart so that I, too, can work for the betterment of all. I pray to accept the challenge of female rule in an effort to change the world for the better.

Mantra for the day

A woman works for all, a man works for himself. A woman works for all, a man works for himself. A woman works for all, a man works for himself.

Reflection for the day

_____

_____

_____

_____

_____

_____

_____

_____

_____

_____

_____

_____

_____

_____

_____

Thought for the day
  I often wonder; just how do people view me? What does my body language say? How is my posture? Do I carry myself well and project a positive image? As I grow to my rightful position in life my body language begins to change. I walk with assurance, head held high, and I meet everyone eye-to-eye. Gone is the self-doubt that was reflected in my movements and language. Gone is the self-deprecating talk that often opened the door to personal attacks by others. These are attacks that I either defended or worse yet; absorbed. I teach people how to treat me. The lesson is this: I am special, I have worth; treat me with the dignity due a self-respecting woman! Today when people look to me they see confidence, they see grace, and my personal worth is reflected in the care I give myself. People are drawn to me because I humbly promote my worth and offer my kindness to others.

Meditation for the day
  Today I envision myself as others see me. What do I need to adjust to properly express my true self? Although I am undergoing great changes, my faith in God allows me to fully exemplify my status as a woman of substance. Today I live as the person I have worked to become. Change is not my enemy, it is my friend.

Prayer for the day
  Just for today; I pray to have all self-doubt removed. I pray that with the power of God and the sisterhood I will 'act as if' in order to become. I pray to have full knowledge of my great worth to my God, my friends, and myself. I pray to become who I really am, who I should have been and what I

will be, self-actuated as an empowered and enlightened woman.

Mantra for the day

     I am responsible for teaching people how to treat me. I am responsible for teaching people how to treat me. I am responsible for teaching people how to treat me.

Reflection for the day

_____

_____

_____

_____

_____

_____

_____

_____

_____

_____

_____

_____

_____

_____

_____

Thought for the day

Men are such crazy creatures but they have a right to be! When we look at the socialization differences between females and males it is easy to see why we often feel a distance when dealing with men. When a male child is little he is held at arms length and often, none too gently, handled and 'bounced'. When it is a little girl, she is held close, gently rocked, loved on and cooed at. Females are socialized with communication skills. Many men are unable to overcome the socialized distance until they come under the tutelage of a patient, warm, passionate woman. Men are taught to compete and conquer, and they try to bring this mindset into the realm of romance. Unfortunately for many men, they must first experience the pains of love before they can break down the emotional walls. This allows them to open their capable hearts and accept the support that an enlightened woman offers. We must always remember that it is the woman who is sought out and desired. In his heart the male knows he will only find true love after he is humbled and the self-protective walls are dismantled.

Meditation for the day

I seek to understand the male distance. I seek to help him transcend his erroneous teachings and become a warm, loving human being. A woman's love is the greatest gift a man will ever experience. As I make the effort to help the willing, I am ever mindful of the ignorant, the mean–spirited and the predator.

Prayer for the day

I pray that my God will enable me to lead men to a new openness with themselves and a new,

closer relationship with people and the world.
Minds and hearts only receive when they are open.

Mantra for the day
     Today I understand their separation. Today I understand their separation. Today I understand their separation.

Reflection for the day

_____

_____

_____

_____

_____

_____

_____

_____

_____

_____

_____

_____

_____

Thought for the day
There are times when I just want to run away. Like a wayward teenager forgetting all the pressures and trouble I look to a magical place where none of the pain or anxiety exist; just start over. I can start over at any time I choose. I don't have to run away or evade the responsibilities I have, whether they are chosen by me or are a consequence of some other life decision. I can change how I perceive these pressures and troubles by focusing on the positive lesson found. It could be the only lesson is that I don't want to do that again or maybe the lesson is much deeper and life changing. Either way, I can change how I see things, find the lesson and face my challenges with the strength of character I have and continue to build. Sometimes we just grow in spite of ourselves.

Meditation for the day
My focus today is on the choices I have in my life today. I can begin my day, my life anew by changing my perception on how I view the challenges that are before me. I have the resources, support and strength needed to face whatever it is that creates feelings of helplessness and anxiety. I reach out to those supports with confidence that allows me to choose wisely.

Prayer for the day
I ask for wisdom and guidance, as always. I ask for courage to face the obstacles in life and use them to my benefit. Please allow the strength I have, through You my God, to benefit other women and display the leadership qualities you would have me share with others.

Mantra for the day

I have the ability to start anew with the choices I make. I have the ability to start anew with the choices I make.

Reflection for the day

_____

_____

_____

_____

_____

_____

_____

_____

_____

_____

_____

_____

_____

_____

_____

_____

_____

Thought for the Day
       Peace! I am seeking a peace-filled existence.
I want to be as free as possible from stress and angst
life can bring. My journey will require much new
thought and compromise on my part, but I must be
mindful not to surrender my core values. Working
for peace does not include self-sacrifice, self-
condemnation or acquiescence of my personal
power. True peace is not found in passive
acceptance. The peace that I seek is found within
my heart and shared with my Maker. When I stand
on my beliefs and work toward my goals with pure
motives, I am able to claim peace as mine, for I will
not compromise my being. Yes I may bend, but I
will not break the covenant that always provides the
level of peace of which I am assured. Peace
through faith is always available to me.

Meditation for the Day
       When I look back I can see that I have found
peace in surrender but never in quiet resignation.
However, when I compromise my beliefs or fail to
stand up for myself I often find turmoil not peace.
Being true to myself and having the courage to
promote my well-being is what provides harmony
in my life. I do not seek peace at any price; I seek
peace with my pride and dignity intact.

Prayer for the Day
       I pray to rightly use the Spirit available to
work for a lifelong peace that I can count on.
Serenity: a calm acceptance that I am willing to
bend to meet the needs of others but I am in no way
willing to compromise my beliefs or my character.
My journey to peace has been long and I will not
back track for someone else's approval.

Mantra for the Day

I possess peace with the dignity of an empowered woman. I possess peace with the dignity of an empowered woman. I possess peace with the dignity of an empowered woman.

Reflection for the day

_____

_____

_____

_____

_____

_____

_____

_____

_____

_____

_____

_____

_____

_____

_____

_____

_____

Thought for the Day

Today I am assured of the strength of my femininity. I have been transformed into a self-assured, enlightened woman of character. I use my newly designed attributes to guide those who share my life. I lead with compassion, truth, and most of all, love. Patriarchy has proven that one cannot lead through mandate. The female leaders of today, and in the days to come, prove that guidance is most effective when accomplished through the positive promotion of the well-being of others. Female empowerment provides for the spiritual nourishment of all parties involved; for it is founded on love. The innate love of the female must be brought to the surface for the benefit of the world. I bring my love fully to life and radiate the compassion that this world has lost.

Meditation for the Day

I no longer sit back as a passive participant in life. I am the Gift and I best express myself through working for the well-being of others. I have my Creator to follow, my sisters to walk with and the willing support of the men in my life. I am free to work for the maximum benefit for myself and my family. An empowered woman shares joyously in the treasures of the heart.

Prayer for the Day

I pray to ever be mindful of the responsibilities that my position demands. I lead as my Creator leads; through kindness, understanding and love. I ask that I remain forever humble in my place of power as a woman.

Mantra for the Day

I am love in action, I am the gift. I am love in action, I am the gift. I am love in action, I am the gift.

Reflection for the day

_____

_____

_____

_____

_____

_____

_____

_____

_____

_____

_____

_____

_____

_____

_____

_____

Thought for the Day
Power lies at the base of all relationships. Generally speaking, one person usually leads while the other party will acquiesce and follow the dictates of the leader. For far too long, I have been the one to give in and follow. As an empowered woman, I now realize that I am free to be the one in power in my personal relationships. Regardless of what our current arrangement is, we can always increase our power and our advantage. All things considered men are relatively uncomplicated. They come to us with a list of wants and desires. It is up to my discretion as to if, when and how these desires are fulfilled. The fact that they seek me out is a clear indication of my power. I understand the strength and wisdom available to me as an enlightened woman. I continue to work for the benefit of myself and my sisters until our superiority is understood and accepted.

Meditation for the Day
Today I take the time to define my strengths and understand his weaknesses. There is no need to be crass or cruel in my rise to power. I am fortified with a superior female mind and heart that desires the best for everyone. Through surrender and acceptance I strengthen emotional connections, enhanced love and a desire for commitment not yet known. When I take the lead, he will follow.

Prayer for the Day
I ask for the strength to honor my commitment to change. I fully recognize that my rise to power will be rift with difficulties and opposition. I pray to meet these challenges with the grace and dignity of an enlightened woman. Belief, decision and action produce the faith I need. As an enlightened woman acts, so shall she be.

Mantra for the Day

The power is mine to control. The power is mine to control. The power is mine to control.

Reflection for the day

_____

_____

_____

_____

_____

_____

_____

_____

_____

_____

_____

_____

_____

_____

_____

_____

_____

_____

Thought for the Day

      Heartache; how we all hate this level of despair. Disappointments, broken hearts, watching those we love suffer. The pain grows deeper with each passing breath. This unwanted, pain-filled visitor feels as if it has come to stay. When we feel this way, we should strive to remember that there are two positives to embrace here; the first is that time heals all wounds and the second is that love is alive. The positive is this; before you can feel pain at this level, you need to be able to love at an equal or greater level. Even though I feel bad, I can be grateful for my ability and capacity to love. I also need to realize that the same love that created my pain delivers my peace once again. Love is endless and ultimately prevails.

Meditation for the Day

      I retrace my emotional footsteps and know that in my inner-most being that love has always and will always deliver me from the pain of heartache. Sometimes I need to refocus, reframe, or redirect my love but it sets me free. When I find myself overcome with the burdens of life, I need to work to enhance my capacity to love selflessly and not to fall into the despair of self-absorption that leads to the blackness of heartache.

Prayer for the Day

      I pray to be able to use love to my advantage. In times of turmoil, I ask to be given the ability to command my love to work positively for myself so others may benefit as well. I believe my Creator wants me to be usefully happy and not trapped in despair, Love creates the wound and love heals the wound.

Mantra for the Day

I will use love to my advantage. I will use love to my advantage. I will use love to my advantage.

Reflection for the day

_____

_____

_____

_____

_____

_____

_____

_____

_____

_____

_____

_____

_____

_____

_____

_____

_____

_____

_____

Thought for the Day

Resistance to tyranny is obedience to God.
-- Susan B. Anthony

I am not recommending wholesale revolution however; it would not hurt to get our priorities straight. I believe that my primary relationship should be a spiritual one. My spirituality is where I find my power, my strength and my hope. Now that I have realized who comes first in my life, I need to ask myself what my Creator would want for me. I believe that the Creative Force would have me as free from societal restraints and the tyranny of others as possible. With spiritual guidance and the help of the sisterhood, I can liberate myself from the pitfalls of societal expectations. In my freedom, I become a willing servant to my Creator and am able to work for the freedom of others.

Meditation for the Day

Today I consider the negative forces in my life and make a plan of action. I rightly gather my thoughts and my resources and begin to work for the change that will bring my liberation. I do not succumb to the tyranny that is often used to manipulate women. I am an enlightened woman and I claim the freedom that my Creator has planned for me.

Prayer for the Day

I pray to pick my battles carefully. I cannot resist everything and everyone that I find offensive, so I must choose wisely and utilize my powers judiciously. Fortified by my faith and loving spirit, I can trust my judgments.

Mantra for the Day

     I resist tyranny and repression. I resist tyranny and repression. I resist tyranny and repression.

Reflection for the day

_____

_____

_____

_____

_____

_____

_____

_____

_____

_____

_____

_____

_____

_____

Thought for the Day

The strong do what they will and the weak suffer what they must. – Thucydides

This statement is about as true as anything can be. I am tired of suffering. It really doesn't matter if it's my fault, their fault or the failings of society as a whole; I'm just tired of it! Therefore in that context, the solution is simple; I need to be strong if I am to stop my discomfort. I live a life of faith instead of fear. All people of faith have strength. I have faith in me, faith in a Higher Power, faith in the people around me. I enhance my beliefs and faith starting right now. I look to my former successes and realize that I can fully expect continued success in the future. I renew my spiritual beliefs and take care of my daily devotions as required. I pick people that I believe in and trust to be in my life. I renounce my former weakness and claim my strength. A queen is strong.

Meditation for the Day

Today is the day that I cast the negativity out for good. I foreswear my victim status and claim my place as hero of my life. I contemplate my new strength and how best to apply it for the benefit of the world. My days of suffering are over.

Prayer for the Day

I pray to change the course of my life. I pray to live in the faith that enables me to claim the strength that is my birthright. I am a woman of substance and will not be denied my proper place in life. I am reborn with a new and stronger spirit.

Mantra for the Day

I have strength, my suffering is over. I have strength, my suffering is over. I have strength, my suffering is over.

Reflection for the day

_____

_____

_____

_____

_____

_____

_____

_____

_____

_____

_____

_____

_____

_____

_____

_____

_____

Thought for the Day

The glory of this day is mine to claim. This is a thought that needs to go with me constantly. I choose my reality, I choose the people that I deal with and I choose to be peacefully content. It has been said that it is hard to be hateful when you are grateful. When I maintain this simple concept of gratitude, my life will continue to respond positively. I have the joy, I have the peace and I have the power. However, these positives can easily be obscured by negativity. When I claim the goodness of the day, when I act on spiritual principles and when I treat myself and others well, there will be no room for oppositional forces. My positive attitude will banish the emotional predators that seek to restrict my positive progress.

Meditation for the Day

I review my life and see where lack of gratitude has slowed my personal ascent. I need not be bothered by the troubles of the world. My life is full of opportunities for growth and gratitude. I express my gratitude with kindness and a helpful attitude toward others. My gratitude will do me no good if I keep it to myself. I will unselfishly share my joy with others.

Prayer for the Day

My most wonderful Creator I come to you in thanks for the joy in my heart. It is through You and Your patience and kindness that I find the faith to banish negativity and claim the gratitude that enables me to present a helpful spirit.

Mantra for the Day

I have an attitude of gratitude. I have an attitude of gratitude. I have an attitude of gratitude.

Reflection for the day

_____

_____

_____

_____

_____

_____

_____

_____

_____

_____

_____

_____

_____

_____

_____

_____

_____

Thought for the day

The secret of happiness is freedom. The secret of freedom is courage. -- Thucydides

I have never connected these three concepts in this fashion before. It looks like I need to go to the back of the line and work my way forward! Courage is the ladder of success, and my courage is founded in my faith. With courage fortified by faith, I seek my freedom and happiness without fail. I cannot sit passively by and wait to be happy or free. These are benefits of hard work, work that can only be done by me. No one can give me freedom; no one can give me happiness. The choices that I make, the courage that I employ and the work that I perform determine the course of my existence. There is no secret to happiness; it is the byproduct of hard work.

Meditation for the day

I thoughtfully employ all of my resources to gain my desired results. I have all of the emotional tools I need to create the life that I desire. No one can stifle my courage, no one can bind my freedom or diminish my happiness. I am queen of my destiny.

Prayer for the day

I pray to be free from doubt. When I remove doubt from my life, I have all the courage that I need. Doubt, turned to fear, succumbs to the courage of my faith. I am sure of my path.

Mantra for the day

Faith, courage, freedom, happiness. Faith, courage, freedom, happiness. Faith, courage, freedom, happiness.

Reflection for the day

_____

_____

_____

_____

_____

_____

_____

_____

_____

_____

_____

_____

_____

_____

_____

_____

Thought for the day

Looking back on life before the changes we
have experienced, it is easy to see that we were
always especially blessed with insight and personal
strength that attracted men with submissive desires.
We may have noticed something different but were
unable to understand what to do or how to handle
the situation. After learning more about female
empowerment and leadership in relationships, we
are able to recognize how to take and shape men to
fulfill their most ardent desire: to serve and worship
a queen, a goddess and meet her needs in a female-
led relationship. As different as it may seem, men
that desire a life of service are able to find as much
fulfillment in their service to a queen as the woman
finds in being served. It's a new world out there
and it is up to the empowered women to strike the
chord of change.

Meditation for the day

Today I look within to find understanding of
the dominant traits I have so long misunderstood. I
focus my energy on ways to increase understanding
for me as well as others in my life. I feel the peace
that comes with understanding and accepting
differences.

Prayer for the day

I pray for continued wisdom and serenity
with the direction of my life. I ask for a humble and
loving heart that brings no pain or shame to those
with different needs than I have accepted as
society's norm. I pray for a loving spirit that will
enhance the lives of others with whom I have the
privilege of sharing my life.

Mantra for the day

I have peace and acceptance for the differences in life. I have peace and acceptance for the differences in life. I have peace and acceptance for the differences in life.

Reflection for the day

_____

_____

_____

_____

_____

_____

_____

_____

_____

_____

_____

_____

_____

_____

_____

_____

Thought for the day

I gleefully claim my full potential. No longer plagued by current doubt or the evil voices of the past, I am free to grow and enjoy the best that this world has to offer. I am queen of my destiny and I bow before no man. I control my heart, my mind and share my soul with my loving Creator. I am as free as I can be. In the past, my mind and my emotions often held me back. I was told that it wasn't my place or I couldn't excel simply based on my gender. My role in life was supposed to be limited by the limited thinking of past generations. Due to my work and the work of the sisterhood, I have become the woman I always knew I could be. I am free at last.

Meditation for the day

Thank goodness for the hard work of the women and men that came before me. Female liberation and power has come with a very high price. Today I reap the benefits of the hard work of my predecessors. I also stand before my Maker and freely acknowledge my willingness and commitment to continue to work for positive change and freedom in the world.

Prayer for the day

Today I offer a simple prayer of thanks for all the hard work of the people that came before me seeking female ascension. The legal battles, the imprisonment, the heartache and self-sacrifice have not been in vain. I, my sisters and the world all enjoy our freedom due to the sacrifice of those God-directed souls that preceded us.

Mantra for the day
    Freedom is never free. Freedom is never
free. Freedom is never free.

Reflection for the day

_____

_____

_____

_____

_____

_____

_____

_____

_____

_____

_____

_____

_____

_____

Thought for the day

Feminism was established to allow unattractive women easier access to the mainstream. -- Rush Limbaugh

I would like it known that I fully support everyone's right to free thought and free speech. However, I seriously doubt that education can or will overcome ignorance or a mean spirit. This is the depth of ignorance that we are going to overcome through the modeling and education of the current and future generations. By being the best women that we can be, we will model empowering behaviors for our coworkers, lovers, and children. Once the chauvinistic dinosaurs pass, a new age of enlightenment will reign supreme upon the land. This is the feminine enlightenment that every woman needs to seek for herself and strive to share with those capable of thought. I thank my loving God that dinosaurs become extinct all by themselves and take their archaic thinking with them.

Meditation for the day

I am grateful to live in a time of change. I can look to the future with assurance that the old patriarchal ways will die and be replaced with the loving spirit of woman. No longer will people's place in society be dictated by their 'unattractiveness' but by their character and compassion. Ignorance and evil, like any other falsehood, will not stand the light of day. Love is the eternal light.

Prayer for the day

I ask for new thought and enlightenment for the mean-spirited people of the world. I humbly request a new age of open-mindedness and cooperation for all. I strive to be an enlightened woman of power and to cast my light upon the shadow of ignorance so that all may benefit from the power of love.

Mantra for the day

I do not brake for dinosaurs. I do not brake for dinosaurs. I do not brake for dinosaurs!

Reflection for the day

_____

_____

_____

_____

_____

_____

_____

_____

_____

_____

_____

LaVergne, TN USA
17 January 2011
212674LV00001B/15/P